Awake
TO HIS
PRESENCE

Harrison House

Shippensburg, PA

TO HIS PRESENCE

THE OPEN DOOR TO THE SECRET PLACE

30 DEVOTIONS WITH GUIDED JOURNAL

KELLIE COPELAND

© Copyright 2023–Kellie Copeland

Printed in the United States of America. All rights reserved. No portion of this book may be reproduced, stored in a retrieval system, or transmitted in any form or by any means—electronic, mechanical, photocopy, recording, scanning, or other—except for brief quotations in critical reviews or articles, without the prior written permission of the publisher.

Scripture quotations marked AMPC are taken from the Amplified® Bible, Classic Edition, Copyright © 1954, 1958, 1962, 1964, 1965, 1987 by The Lockman Foundation. All rights reserved. Used by permission.

Scripture quotations marked AMP are taken from the Amplified® Bible, Copyright © 2015 by The Lockman Foundation, La Habra, CA 90631. All rights reserved. Used by permission.

Scripture quotations marked NKJV are taken from the New King James Version. Copyright © 1982 by Thomas Nelson, Inc. Used by permission. All rights reserved.

Scripture quotations marked NLT are taken from the Holy Bible, New Living Translation, copyright 1996, 2004, 2015. Used by permission of Tyndale House Publishers, Wheaton, Illinois 60189. All rights reserved.

Scripture quotations marked TPT are taken from *The Passion Translation*, Copyright © 2017, 2018, 2020 by Passion & Fire Ministries, Inc., www.thepassiontranslation.com. Used by permission of BroadStreet Publishing Group, LLC, Racine, Wisconsin, USA. All rights reserved.

Scripture quotations marked TLV are taken from the Tree of Life Translation of the Bible, Copyright © 2015 by The Messianic Jewish Family Bible Society. Used by permission. All rights reserved.

Scripture quotations marked NIV are taken from the HOLY BIBLE, NEW INTERNATIONAL VERSION®, Copyright © 1973, 1978, 1984, 2011 International Bible Society. Used by permission of Zondervan. All rights reserved.

Scripture quotations marked MSG are taken from *The Message*. Copyright © 1993, 1994, 1995, 1996, 2000, 2001, 2002. Used by permission of NavPress Publishing Group.

Published by Harrison House Publishers
Shippensburg, PA 17257

ISBN 13 TP: 978-1-6803-1839-5

ISBN 13 eBook: 978-1-6803-1840-1

ISBN 13 HC: 978-1-6803-1842-5

ISBN 13 LP: 978-1-6803-1841-8

For Worldwide Distribution, Printed in the U.S.A.

1 2 3 4 5 6 7 8 / 27 26 25 24 23

Dedication

This book is dedicated to my tribe, my precious family. They love me, encourage me, stand up for me and inspire me every day. They are my biggest cheerleaders and most ardent fans, always ready with a thoughtful and honest opinion.

I love my children and grandchildren and consider them to be the greatest gifts I've ever been given. Thank You, Lord, for such perfect gifts.

Rachel and Caleb Mayer
and children
Kenneth, Katherine and Clark Mayer

Lyndsey and Alex Torres
and daughter
Colette Torres

Jenny and Elias Papapostolou
and son
Andreas Papapostolou

Max and Madi Kutz

Emily Swisher

Acknowledgements

There would be no book had Jesus not awakened me! So, I want to first thank Him for His love and pursuit of my heart. I didn't know He was writing a book when He was writing on my heart. Thank You, my precious Jesus.

I want to say thank you to my family. My children have walked with me through this process and made invaluable contributions, each in their own way. Rachel, your cover design captured the heart of the invitation I hoped to deliver. Max, you captured the photos beautifully and made the shoot so easy and comfortable. Lyndsey, you are a gifted writer and editor. You brought such clarity to the manuscript. Jenny and Emily, you set the mood and inspiration I needed to focus and get to work more than once. The candles and yule log video on the TV did the trick to bring instant atmosphere!

I want to thank my parents, Kenneth and Gloria Copeland, for being the best parents, teachers, friends and shepherds imaginable. It was at your feet that I learned to love the Lord and to live by uncompromising faith in the Word of God, no matter the circumstances. That way of life took me to His feet when circumstances were too much to bear. That's where I fell even more in love with Jesus. You were the open door to Heaven on earth with Him. Thank you forever to my favorite preachers in the world.

To my best friend, Kim Stephenson, thank you for just always being there for me. To work, minister, play and produce with your best friend is just the love and favor of God. He knew just the right person to send to both value and support me while at the same time challenge me. Everyone should have a Kim in their life. Laverne and Shirley, Lucy and Ethel and Kim and Kellie, enough said....

Thank you to the Harrison House and Nori Media Group team who have been so gracious, kind and encouraging during this process. From the first conversation with Kyle Loffelmacher and Brad Herman telling me I had a message from the Lord, they have supported me in every step. Thank you for your patience and listening ear as I consistently talk too much when we meet. You were indispensable, and I'm grateful to call you friends.

Thank you to Kaye Mountz, editor supreme! You are anointed to make sense and bring clarity and catch mistakes. Working with you was like working with the Holy Spirit directly! He flows from you so mightily.

Thank you to the other amazing friends at Destiny Image and Nori Media Group for welcoming me to your beautiful circle. Tina Pugh, Larry Sparks and Cavet Leibensperger, you befriended me and opened doors to new worlds of opportunity, revelation and outpouring to me. I'm so grateful.

Lastly, I have grown up with wonderful mentors and teachers in my life whose ministries have changed millions of people's lives. I am grateful for their contribution to me, and they will always be precious in my eyes. There are many, but I want to mention: Kenneth and Gloria Copeland, Jerry and Carolyn Savelle, Creflo and Taffi Dollar, Jesse and Cathy Duplantis, Keith and Phyllis Moore, Bill and Veronica Winston and Rick and Denise Renner. You helped build a strong foundation of the Word of God. Thank you for all you do. Never quit pressing and preaching the uncompromised word! Billions more need to hear it!

In the last few years, the Lord has added precious new voices in my life to impart new depths of His Love and presence and deliverance. I want to name a few who have greatly impacted my life: Bill and Beni Johnson, Katie Souza, Robert Henderson, Michael and Jess Koulianos, Todd and Jackie White, Christine Caine, Suzanne and Benny Hinn and Francis Chan.

I'm also eternally grateful to all the worship houses and ministers of music who led me into a deeper worship of Jesus. I needed someone to follow, and you were there.

There are too many other impactful individuals and ministries to mention them all, but Heaven knows your name, and I ask that your reward be great for all you've done for His people.

I must thank Brian Simmons for allowing his life to be caught up in The Passion Translation. You did more than translate the Bible. You allowed the Holy Spirit to pierce our souls by opening our thoughts to His "wrap-around" presence. Thank you!

Thank you, dear reader, for being willing to take this journey with me. You are the co-author of the book you hold in your hands, and therefore, no two versions will be the same. My prayer is that your life will be an unusual expression of His love and faithfulness.

PSALM 25

(TPT)

Always I will lift up my soul into your presence, Yahweh.
Be there for me, my God, for I keep trusting in you.
Don't allow my foes to gloat over me or
the shame of defeat to overtake me.
Could anyone be disgraced
when he has entwined his heart with yours?
But my foes will all be defeated and ashamed
when they harm the innocent.
Direct me, Yahweh, throughout my journey
so I can experience your plans for my life.
Reveal the life-paths that are pleasing to you.
Escort me into your truth; take me by the hand and teach me.
For you are the God of my salvation;
I have wrapped my heart into yours all day long!
Forgive my failures as a young man,
and overlook the sins of my immaturity.
Give me grace, Yahweh! Always look at me
through your eyes of love—
your forgiving eyes of mercy and compassion.

When you think of me, see me as one you love and care for.
How good you are to me!
When people turn to you, Yahweh,
they discover how easy you are to please—so faithful and true!
Joyfully you teach them the proper path,
even when they go astray.
Keep showing the humble your path,
and lead them into the best decision.
Bring revelation-light that trains them in the truth.
Loving are all the ways of Yahweh, loving and faithful for
those who keep his covenant.
For the honor of your name, Yahweh,
never count my many sins, and forgive them all—
lift their burden off of my life!
Who are they that live in the holy fear of Yahweh?
You will show them the right path to take.
Then prosperity and favor will be their portion,
and their descendants will inherit the earth.
There's a private place reserved for the
devoted lovers of Yahweh,
where they sit near him and receive
the revelation-secrets of his promises.
Rescue me, Yahweh, for you free my feet from every trap.
Sorrows fill my heart as I feel helpless, mistreated—
I'm all alone and in misery!
Come closer to me now, for I need your mercy.

*Turn to me, for my problems seem to
be going from bad to worse.
Only you can free me from all these troubles!
Until you lift this burden, the burden of all my sins,
my troubles and trials will be more than I can handle.
Can't you feel my pain?
Vicious, violent enemies hate me.
There are so many, Lord. Can't you see?
Will you protect me from their power against
me? I have taken shelter in you.
Let it never be said that when I trusted you,
you didn't come to my rescue.
Your perfection and faithfulness are my bodyguards,
for you are my hope and I trust in you as my only protection.
Zealously, God, we ask you
to come save Israel from all her troubles,
for you provide the ransom price for your people!*

CONTENTS

Wrap Your Heart into His **17**

A Road Map for the Encounters Ahead **39**

Encounter 1	I Am Awakened 41
Encounter 2	An Invitation to the Throne Room 47
Encounter 3	Things to Come 51
Encounter 4	Good Morning 57
Encounter 5	Wait for Me 65
Encounter 6	Be on Assignment 71
Encounter 7	My House 77
Encounter 8	Come In 83
Encounter 9	Grace and Favor 89
Encounter 10	Face to Face 95
Encounter 11	This Is Me 101
Encounter 12	Gaze Deeply 107
Encounter 13	Our Joy 115
Encounter 14	Perfect Love 121

Encounter 15	Take and Eat Communion	129
Encounter 16	Days of Heaven	137
Encounter 17	A New Day	143
Encounter 18	Living *in* Me	149
Encounter 19	Look to Me	155
Encounter 20	I Am Your Savior	161
Encounter 21	Trust Me	167
Encounter 22	My Secret Garden	173
Encounter 23	Perfect Security	181
Encounter 24	Helping You	189
Encounter 25	Family Love	197
Encounter 26	Light and Life	205
Encounter 27	The Long Walk	211
Encounter 28	Light Therapy	219
Encounter 29	The Press	227
Encounter 30	Gateway of Hope	235

The Blank Lines Ahead **241**

Ask Jesus into Your Heart **253**

About the Author **254**

WRAP YOUR HEART INTO HIS

Awaken! It's all about awakening. This is what Jesus did for me. Tenderly and progressively, His presence drew me closer to Him until I was changed. The greatness of the change in my life that came from sitting with Him truly can't be put into words. Instead of trying to put the whole of my experience in front of you, I invite you to enter His presence where you can experience Him for yourself. He's waiting for *you!*

After completing the 30 encounters of guided moments on the pages that follow, I sat down to write to you from my heart. I wanted to tell you how Jesus has given me promises, help and insight into the Kingdom. There was so much I wanted to say that it overwhelmed me. I heard the Lord's heart as He said, "It's too much," and I agreed.

Clarity came as I spent time with Him. He said, "Keep it simple. Our most amazing interactions occur when you are simply in My presence, knowing Me as Emmanuel."

Keeping it simple requires us to acknowledge that Jesus is the Shepherd, the One with the complicated, multi-dimensional role to play in our lives. He's the One who planned our existence long ago. He knows our heart, and He's always aware of our condition.

Psalm 139:1-18 (TPT)

Lord, you know everything there is to know about me.
You perceive every movement of my heart and soul,

*and you understand my every thought
before it even enters my mind.*
You are so intimately aware of me, Lord.
*You read my heart like an open book
and you know all the words I'm about to speak
before I even start a sentence!*
You know every step I will take before my journey even begins.
*You've gone into my future to prepare the way,
and in kindness you follow behind me to
spare me from the harm of my past.*
You have laid your hand on me!
This is just too wonderful, deep, and incomprehensible!
Your understanding of me brings me wonder and strength.
*Where could I go from your Spirit? Where
could I run and hide from your face?*
If I go up to heaven, you're there!
If I go down to the realm of the dead, you're there too!
If I fly with wings into the shining dawn, you're there!
If I fly into the radiant sunset, you're there waiting!
*Wherever I go, your hand will guide me;
your strength will empower me.*
*It's impossible to disappear from you or
to ask the darkness to hide me,*
for your presence is everywhere, bringing light into my night.
*There is no such thing as darkness with you.
the night, to you, is as bright as the day;
there's no difference between the two.*

*You formed my innermost being, shaping my
delicate inside and my intricate outside,*

and wove them all together in my mother's womb.

I thank you, God, for making me so mysteriously complex!

Everything you do is marvelously breathtaking.

It simply amazes me to think about it!

How thoroughly you know me, Lord!

*You even formed every bone in my body when
you created me in the secret place;*

carefully, skillfully you shaped me from nothing to something.

You saw who you created me to be before I became me

*Before I'd ever seen the light of day, the
number of days you planned for me*

were already recorded in your book.

Every single moment you are thinking of me!

*How precious and wonderful to consider that you
cherish me constantly in your every thought!*

*O God, your desires toward me are more than
the grains of sand on every shore!*

When I awake each morning, you're still with me.

The simple beauty of life with Jesus becomes more evident and real when we keep our part simple. Though it seems like we would experience more if we work harder, the opposite is true. So, remember to give Him your KISS (keep it so simple) as you sit with Him.

ALLURE

I have found the power to *be* simple also comes from Him! There is a secret process in Hosea 2:14-16 that expresses His powerful part of our ability to come to Him.

> *"Therefore, behold, I will allure her, bring her into the wilderness and speak kindly to her. I will return her vineyards to her and transform the Valley of Trouble into a gateway of hope. She will give herself to me there, as she did long ago when she was young, when I freed her from her captivity in Egypt. When that day comes," says the Lord, "you will call me 'my husband', instead of 'my master.'"*
>
> Hosea 2:14-16
> (verse 14 NASB1995, verses 15-16 TPT)

The word *allure* as used in verse 14 means "to be wide open, spacious, especially in a mental sense, to *cause* to be simple." That is eye opening! The meaning of the word *wilderness* surprised me too. It means "a pasture or open field for feeding flocks." *And*, it also means "a mouth, as an organ of speech."

God is calling you to a wide-open place with Him where you will simply follow and feed on the words of the Shepherd, face to face. His very breath, *ruach* in Hebrew, means to infuse strength as He speaks. The deeper into His wilderness experience you go, the more His Words and His presence take on a new importance in your life. They become louder than any circumstance you may be walking through. You will begin to know Him as intimately as a spouse instead of just religiously following orders.

Remember, when Jesus was *led* into the wilderness by the Spirit in Luke 4:1-16? Why would the Holy Spirit do that? Jesus *needed* to be in that place of open pasture in the Spirit, being fed words from the Father that would carry Him into His destiny and ultimate victory. When Satan came to tempt Him, all that Word came pouring out in power and sent the enemy running as Jesus repeatedly said, "It is written!" It really wasn't Jesus being tested but the power of the Word being proven as Jesus held fast to God's words. Mark 4:15 exposes the device Satan used on Jesus in the wilderness, which is the root of *every* device the enemy uses on us too.

Mark 4:15 (NKJV) says:

> *And these are the ones by the wayside where the word is sown. When they hear, Satan comes immediately and takes away the word that was sown in their hearts.*

Luke 4:14 (AMPC) tells us the rest of the story as Jesus defeated Satan with the Word of God:

> *Then Jesus went back full of and under the power of the [Holy] Spirit into Galilee....*

Jesus came out of that experience full of power and led by the Spirit, knowing that the Word of God has the power to defeat the enemy *and* bring the comfort and help needed in His soul and body. This was not just a theory of words but had become His experience! In this important encounter, Jesus' authority over the enemy and His future victory over death were established forever.

Friend, you and I need to be grounded and established in God's words as well. And Jesus is here to help us. He will feed us words from the heart of the Father that will carry us into our destiny and victory, giving us hope and healing along the way.

A ROYAL INVITATION

The King of Heaven has issued an official invitation into His presence. He literally invites you in His Word to come to Him. You will find these moments of invitation all over the Bible, so why would He not invite you to come to Him *now?*

How simple is it to accept an invitation! You need only to show up to experience what has been prepared for you, and here you are. If simple has not been your experience in the past when you tried to hear from the Lord, consider these possible roadblocks.

First, as we have seen with Jesus' experience, Satan is a liar and comes to steal the Word immediately. Stealing the Word is how he kills and destroys. The Word is his number-one target—not your life, family or health or finances. If he can steal the Word that the Lord is speaking to you, he can take anything Jesus promised you out of your hands.

Satan is the enemy of our souls, and he has deceived us into thinking it's hard to hear from the Lord. We've made hearing about our goodness and abilities, not the goodness and full capability of our Shepherd. We've made it about our faithfulness and level of spiritual maturity—not His.

When you read those statements, they sound ridiculous, don't they?

Since when is the immaturity of a child and his or her inability to hear more important than the wisdom and mature ability of the adult to speak in a manner the child understands?

It's not our desire to make His job harder. We love Him, and we believe Him. So, what's the disconnect between this love and hearing Him express His love? We've distrusted ourselves and what we are hearing, thinking it's just our own random thoughts.

Speaking of our own random thoughts, let's talk about our "prayers." We have this human propensity to go to God in prayer, asking Him for His help or spending our prayer time *telling Him* what and who He needs to change in order to help us. I'll let that thought drop right there. (It was a big ouch for me!) Prayer should be a two-way communication where we not only share our hearts but also receive God's great wisdom for us. Beyond that, His words contain power to bring themselves to pass (Luke 1:37 AMPC). It is a disconnect for our faith when we don't give Him the time and quiet to speak His mighty words of truth and wisdom back to us.

FAITH

Faith comes when He speaks directly to our hearts. Romans 10:17 (NASB95) says, "So faith *comes* from hearing, and hearing by the word of Christ."

The Greek word used in this verse for *word* is *rhema,* which means "spoken word." So then faith comes from hearing and hearing through the spoken word. In sitting with the Lord and experiencing the power of hearing Him *inside* my soul, I realized the true meaning of Hebrews 12:2:

> *We do this by keeping our eyes on Jesus, the champion who initiates and perfects our faith…*(NLT).

Jesus initiates or authors our faith when we hear Him speak and faith comes supernaturally in that moment! We have real access to His thoughts about us, our situations and our destinies.

When we spend time with Him, we discover He is not indifferent but involved in every detail of our lives.

This is not the end of His promise to us. He is the author, initiator, perfector and the developer of our faith.

Connect that back to Romans 10:17 once again and the meaning becomes so clear: Faith is born in us by hearing His spoken Word, and it is developed and perfected as we hear Him speak again and again. Pause and think about this for a minute! This is the life-changing definition of the Good Shepherd. As Jesus develops our faith, we have the power and courage to keep walking forward, holding onto what He says about us and what He's promised to us.

One more golden nugget to add here is found in Hebrews 6:17-20 (NLT).

> *God also bound himself with an oath, so that those who received the promise could be perfectly sure that he would never change his mind. So God has given both his promise and his oath. These two things are unchangeable because it is impossible for God to lie. Therefore, we who have fled to him for refuge can have great confidence as we hold to the hope that lies before us. This hope is a strong and trustworthy anchor for our souls. It leads us through the curtain into God's inner sanctuary. Jesus has already gone in there for us. He has become our eternal High Priest in the order of Melchizedek.*

With every word of promise God speaks to us, He's bound Himself with an oath, and it is *impossible for Him to lie!* (Numbers 23:19).

Do you see the power of hearing His promises spoken directly to your heart? He is bound by His own Word that He cannot lie. We've had a promise and an oath from almighty God all this time, and yet, we've been trudging along, trying to walk out our Christian life without His hand-holding. It reminds me of trying to keep my children from breaking our handhold in a crowded amusement park. How many times do we pull away, trying to figure out which way to go when He is there to lead us faithfully through?

Recently, when He showed me this truth, I was pressing into a promise He had given me. I realized I had an oath to go along with the promise when He said, "I am your Shepherd. Hold one hand like it's My promise and the other like it's My oath." I could so picture Him walking me to the manifestation of what He had promised me.

THE TABLE

When you and I stop "adulting" with Jesus, He can be our Good Shepherd, provider, peace and whatever-we-need Savior. Oh how wonderful to be a simple sheep! This is truly the power of Psalm 23. We have heard this beautiful scripture as a word of peace, which it is, but let's acknowledge the mighty power it represents in these promises to those who will follow Him. He will make us lie down in a new pasture filled with the words we need every day, a new daily bread for each day's challenges and blessings! He will hold us and guide us through the specter of death and trouble with His rod of correction and rescue. If He is truly our Shepherd, we shall not want for *any* good thing! He restores our very life and makes our soul new again.

> *You prepare a table before me in the presence of my enemies;*
> *You anoint my head with oil; My cup runs over.*
> Psalm 23:5 (NKJV)

I think we are divinely tired of spending our existence seeking ways to satisfy those wants. Some wants are obvious—those connected to relationships, finances, health, joy, peace, quality of life and comfort. We go about life working, living and seeking entertainment as we try to make ourselves and those around us happy. Other less obvious motives like acceptance, value, validation, power and relief from unseen hurts or trauma prevent us from fulfilling our core desire, which is simply to *belong*.

> *You were like sheep that continually wandered away, but now you have returned to the **true** Shepherd of your lives— the **kind** Guardian who **lovingly** watches over your souls.*
>
> 1 Peter 2:25 (TPT)

He has prepared a table for us, a covenant table in the presence of our enemies. Could our enemies be the lies Satan has planted in our souls? Yes! Jesus will expose and destroy those enemies at this covenant table until His anointing fills us and overflows out of us. He surrounds us with His mercy and unfailing love, forever assuring us that we indeed *belong* to Him.

Revelation 3:20 (TPT) talks about this table:

> *Behold, I'm standing at the door, knocking. If your heart is open to hear my voice and you open the door within, I will come in to you and feast with you, and you will feast with me.*

We are living in the days of Revelation 1-3, the glorious unveiling of Jesus Christ. The book of Revelation opens with the expression of who Jesus is and was and is to come. Then, we receive the invitation to hear the love and correction Jesus speaks to us, the Church. I love this invitation to not only respond to His knocking and open the door of our hearts to Him but also to invite Him to come in and sit down, allowing Him to sift through our hearts.

Revelation 2:23b (TPT) says:

> ...*I am the one who thoroughly searches the most secret thought and the innermost being....*

In essence, after searching the heart condition of the churches, Jesus gives them a diagnosis. He says to them, "I love this about you but not that; I put this other great truth in you, and I am lighting it on fire if you will let me burn the other out." Maybe this is a simplistic view of this Revelation given to John, but it has helped me to not only see an open seat at the table but also to sit down and let Him search my heart. As He has slowly sifted through, He's healed my heart, all the while inflaming my love for Him, my passion for the Kingdom and my love for others. Out of previously barren ground, He has brought fruit, and I am beginning to know Him as the Vine Keeper that He describes in John 15.

I feel confident in saying that in your conversations with Jesus, He will bring needed correction to you as He did so lovingly with me. I pray you will realize that His great love is the backdrop that unfolds as He prunes away the dark places in your life.

Romans 1 tells us that God is at war with every form of sin. He is not at war with us but with the sin in our hearts that causes evil actions. Jesus has come to free us! Hear His love as He works to rid you of your troubles—inside and out. He doesn't expect you to rid yourself of sin so you can enter His presence. This is not true in the least! He welcomes you to come as you are! He invites you to come with your burdens as the song "Just as I Am" says:

> *Just as I am, without one plea*
> *But that Thy blood was shed for me*
> *And that Thou bid'st me come to Thee*
> *Oh, Lamb of God, I come, I come.*[1]

You've worked too hard for too long, and it's time to accept His invitation to sit at the table in the empty chair reserved for you. He will tell you who you are—that you *are* valuable and you *already* belong. I know He will do this because it's His actual job and destiny as the Son of God. He came as the perfect expression of the Father's love for *you*.

SIMPLY COME

So how do we keep it simple with Jesus? We do *our* part vs. *do* our part. See the subtle but critical difference? If we can wrap our busy selves around *our* part, doing it would not be so hard.

One piece of drawing closer to Him is our availability. The Lord ministered these words to my daughter, Rachel, "Your progress is not your responsibility. Your responsibility is availability." That just blew a hole in some of our behaviors, didn't it? But it makes sense that if He is leading us, then we progress when we are available to be led. Availability doesn't require greatness on our part—simply a humble awareness of our need for Him.

When we become concerned about our progress, the good virtue of patient endurance leading to excellence of maturity can instead easily become a works-based life of performance. This only leads to a self-made perfection, which is, perhaps, the furthest thing God wants from us. This is a counterfeit to real, true spiritual growth that leads to His perfection being formed in us. Can you see how this lie bleeds into our "trying" to hear His voice?

In this scenario, we begin to believe it is our own perfection and spiritual maturity that causes our Father to want to speak to us—or not speak to us. This is a requirement we impose upon ourselves.

Remember! God's perfection is sure. Our perfection is not *required* to *sit* at the table; instead, our perfection is actually *acquired* while we are *seated* at the table with Him.

Ironically, when we think we must be perfect, we are too busy working out our so-called perfection to actually sit down. This creates an endless religious cycle that goes nowhere but gradually descends into hopelessness. We think we are walking by faith and trying to stay steady on our scriptures but, all the while, we've become shipwrecked by putting our faith in ourselves and not in Him.

What is the way out of this cycle? We must trust Jesus' ability and spiritual maturity to know how to speak to us and be heard by us *more* than we *dis*trust ourselves. It's that simple. And yet, it's profoundly true. To believe God's truth is to *experience* His freedom and His promises.

Try this! Really! Do it! Don't just read about it (maybe that is what is wrong in the first place).

Get ready to experience an important moment. But first, if you've never asked Jesus into your heart, flip to the back of this book to page 253 and pray the short prayer inviting Jesus to come into your heart, and He will. Again, it's so simple. Then come back to experience this moment with Him:

Put your hand over your chest or belly, whichever feels to you like you are recognizing His Spirit in you.

Close your eyes and focus on Jesus.

Say this out loud:

"*I love You, Jesus.*"

Then, be quiet and just listen!

Ready, go....

What did you hear?

If your answer is "nothing," think again.

Did words quickly come back to you? Did you dismiss them as being your own thoughts?

When I do this with children, it's always fun because they are the easiest group to lead. They hear something and just naturally believe it's Jesus. They hear Him say all kinds of things like, "I love you too!" "You are going to have a great day!" or "I'm proud of you!" He seems to stick to the pretty simple phrase of "I love you too" with adults. Maybe it's all we can handle at first.

I often open up my conversations with Jesus, saying, "I love You, Jesus." He always says, "I love you too." Often, He adds my name to His declaration. Many times, He will just keep right on talking afterward.

This has been a wonderful way to introduce my children and grandchildren to His loving voice. One night, I said to my daughter, "Emily, let's talk to Jesus. One, two, three," and she said with me," I love You, Jesus."

To me, Jesus said the simple, "I love you too." But Emily kept her eyes closed longer and was intently listening. I grew impatient to see how it turned out and asked her, "What did He say?"

She looked at me with annoyance on her face and said, "Shhh, you're interrupting Him!" and went back to listening. If we could be so childlike, oh, the wonders we would hear!

EMMANUEL, GOD WITH US

What a beautiful open door for all of us to experience His love. Jesus is the miracle of Emmanuel, God with us, and He wants His love to be experienced in reality, not in mere words alone.

Ephesians 3:14-19 (TPT) proves this to be His will:

> *So I kneel humbly in awe before the Father of our Lord Jesus, the Messiah, the perfect Father of every father and child in heaven and on the earth. And I pray that he would unveil within you the unlimited riches of his glory and favor until supernatural strength floods your innermost being with his divine might and explosive power. Then, by constantly using your faith, the life of Christ will be released deep inside you, and the resting place of his love will become the very source and root of your life. Then you will be empowered to discover what every holy one experiences—the great magnitude of the astonishing love of Christ in all its dimensions.*
>
> *How deeply intimate and far-reaching is his love! How enduring and inclusive it is!*
>
> *Endless love beyond measurement that transcends our understanding—this extravagant love pours into you until you are filled to overflowing with the fullness of God!*

When we stop believing the lie of the enemy that says, "Those were just your thoughts," we can believe what we heard so quickly spoken in our hearts was, indeed, the voice of our Lord.

When we invite Jesus to speak with us, we are responding in faith to His invitation to come. Would the Good Shepherd of our soul let the enemy of our soul have access to the space between us? Would

He stay silent when we answer His call, allowing Satan to imitate Him? No and no.

John 10:1-5 (NLT) says:

> "I tell you the truth, anyone who sneaks over the wall of a sheepfold, rather than going through the gate, must surely be a thief and a robber! But the one who enters through the gate is the shepherd of the sheep. The gatekeeper opens the gate for him, and the sheep recognize his voice and come to him. He calls his own sheep by name and leads them out. After he has gathered his own flock, he walks ahead of them, and they follow him because they know his voice. They won't follow a stranger; they will run from him because they don't know his voice."

I believe we can live in the Spirit—in our Lord's presence—to the degree that Satan cannot get a word in edgewise as they say in Texas. If Satan can't speak to us because we won't listen, he won't be able to plant lies in our hearts anymore! This is the powerful and peaceful result of giving Jesus full reign over our souls.

Now, go back and try that conversation starter with Jesus again. This time with a new faith in your heart and a purposeful trust in the Good Shepherd, the gatekeeper and King of your soul.

I am confident that you heard Him respond because it's what He does!

Psalm 78:1-2 (KJV) says:

> **Give ear,** O my people, to my law [teaching]; incline your ears to the words of my mouth. I will open my mouth in a parable [in instruction by numerous examples]; I will utter dark sayings of old [that hide important truth].

You are on your journey with Him already. Trust Him to be your Teacher and Friend, to shine light on His sayings to you even as you read His Word in His Presence.

Worship Him as you sit with Him. This is a crucial piece of relationship with Jesus—not only in your journal time but in all your time with Him.

Worship is not just something you do, but it is a posture and positioning of your heart.

You speak worship every time you choose His Word over your circumstances. You exemplify worship as you obey Him, and you beautifully worship Him as you sing the words of spiritual songs from your heart. As you express yourself to Him, you are humbling yourself before Him and aligning your soul in submission to His greatness. As you sing, you are declaring to your mind, will and emotions that He is God Almighty—you are not.

He becomes bigger to you while you begin to recognize the rested peace of being small, cared for and loved—truly loved by Him. In His presence in true worship, you become aware that you can be real with Him, sharing all your thoughts and cares, and He will listen to you. He is so kind as to use your times of worship to tell you who *you* are *in Him*.

This is Jesus, our human Son of God and Son of Man in one. God and Man in us and One with us. We have no idea who we really are until we hear it straight from Jesus. I heard my friend, Grace, say a profound thing: "Our identity is found in His Voice."

He knows how to be heard, and He invited us to simply come, expecting to hear. Jesus admonished the 12 disciples, the multitudes and the Church repeatedly from Matthew to Revelation with these words, "If any have ears to hear, let him hear." He offered us promise after promise of what we can expect as we hear, believe and do His will. My prayer for you is that you may have ears to hear.

MY HOPES FOR YOU

My hope is that you will remove any roadblock that would hinder you from hearing. I have so many hopes for you as you begin to sit with Jesus and spend time with Him, they could fill another chapter. But again, I'll keep it simple. I hope you approach this book with excitement at the experience ahead of you.

I hope you don't pay any attention to the "30-day" format. If a day can be to the Lord as a thousand years, then a day can be two hours or two weeks to you. Take your time as you go through the conversations and encounters with Him. He may have so much to say to you, or you to Him, that your conversation fills pages. It will be wonderful and life-changing!

Conversely, I hope you don't feel duty bound to do this every day. Rather, let your delight in His presence drive you to sit with Him again. My hunger for Him began to demand fewer and fewer days between each encounter. Amazingly, He had something to say whenever I would sit myself down with an ear to hear and a pen to write. I hope you continue to press in, until one day you realize that the times in His presence don't stop when you put your journal down, but He continues to speak to you as you go about your day.

I hope you don't allow the blank lines or lack of space in this journal to pressure or intimidate you. You can also keep a journal or use the blank pages in the back to record what He says when there are no lines or not enough lines. This is *your* conversation with Him not to be dictated by lines. This journal is your invitation to freedom, not a box to imprison you!

I believe that out of your experience in His presence, you will begin to understand the heart behind Psalm 84:10-12 (TPT). This whole psalm expresses this joy!

> *For just one day of intimacy with you is like*
> *a thousand days of joy rolled into one!*
> *I'd rather stand at the threshold in front of the Gate Beautiful,*
> *ready to go in and worship my God,*
> *than to live my life without you*
> *in the most beautiful palace of the wicked.*
> *For the Lord God is brighter than the brilliance of a sunrise!*
> *Wrapping himself around me like a shield,*
> *he is so generous with his gifts of grace and glory.*
> *Those who walk along his paths with integrity*
> *will never lack one thing they need, for he provides it all!*
> *O Lord of Heaven's Armies, what euphoria fills those*
> *who forever trust in you!*

He is our Shepherd and the Lord of Heaven's armies. He is our hope and our overwhelming victory. He has more hopes for you than I can mention or know, and He is ready to work and weave them into your past, your now and your future. You think you're sitting peacefully with the Shepherd as He comforts you, but suddenly you realize the Lord of Heaven's armies just fought your battle and handed it to you on a platter. That's our Jesus, and it's how He works His hopes in you. As you sit with Him, you will hear the faithfulness and the love on one hand and His mighty power to slay your enemies on the other!

IT'S TIME

As you open the door of your heart to Him, realize you are headed to another door that's been standing open and waiting for you.

> *After these things I looked, and behold, a door was standing open in heaven. And the first voice, which I had heard speaking with me like a trumpet, said, "Come up here, and I will show you what must take place after these things." Immediately I was in the Ruach; and behold, a throne was standing in heaven, and One seated on the throne.*
>
> Revelation 4:1-2 (TLV)

The scripture says, "Immediately I was in the *Ruach*" or breath of God. My friend, find your rest there. Find His peace there.

"What if I don't hear anything?" someone might ask. Let the questions fade away, face to face in His presence. Just be still. Wait on the Lord. He can do more with five minutes of quiet than we can do with thousands of years of words. Wait like a pregnant mother waits—waiting not because nothing is happening but because everything is happening. She waits in expectancy! As you sit with Him, His wonderful Holy Spirit will hover over you as He did Mary, confirming His Word with His presence and with signs following. This was His plan all along. So be seated, knowing that His desire is to be with you as your Guide into the very throne of God. He's inviting you and welcoming you as He says, "Come, sit with Me."

It all begins with a simple *"Yes, Lord...."*

NOTE

1. "Just as I Am," lyrics by Charlotte Elliott (1789-1871), music by William Batchelder Bradbury (1816-1868). Public domain.

A ROAD MAP FOR THE ENCOUNTERS AHEAD

As you begin the encounters on the pages that follow, you will discover messages from Jesus that will draw you into a deeper communication and intimate relationship with Him. Included are tools to inspire heart-to-heart conversations between the two of you.

Each entry includes:

- An opening text scripture for meditation
- A message from Jesus in quotes "" that was collected from my conversations with Him but apply to us all!
- Responses from me in *italics* to help guide the conversation
- Lines to write the words of Jesus as He speaks to you
- Prompts and lines for you to write the responses resonating in your heart as you freely talk to Jesus
- Scriptures included for optional meditation and study as you process His Word in His presence

The door is open! He's waiting! Come *awake in His presence*...

Encounter 1

> …"*Awake, sleeper, and arise from the dead, and Christ will shine [as dawn] upon you and give you light.*"
>
> **Ephesians 5:14 (AMP)**

I AM AWAKENED

> Waking up is hard to do. It takes courage and accessibility to allow Me entrance into your life, to make Me the Lord of your life. I have come to be LORD of your life.
>
> I come. You're drawing close to Me when you respond. That is why it's important to structure your time to allow Me to move. Many times, I've sought your presence, but you were not available. You were not home when I knocked. Your busyness and your lifestyle have shut Me out. This is why I must knock.
>
> Should I have to knock on the door of a heart that belongs to Me? Certainly not! This is My territory. This is My land. So, make it a point to open the door. Then, when I come in, I will not leave.
>
> Wake up! Do it supernaturally! In our times together, we'll discuss many things. If I can't come in, you won't see Me.

Kellie: *I'm awake!*

Jesus says to me...

> Working with you is My preferred method of reaching others. Living through you is My greatest impact. Offer yourself to Me, and you will be equipped to offer Me to the world.

Kellie: *Lord, You'll have to help me. That sounds out of my reach.*

Jesus, right now I feel...

> Do you think I am out of your reach? I have made Myself available. Come to Me, and I will give you what you need—the needs you know and the needs you are unaware of. This will be glorious, but the greater glory will be found in abiding. For in abiding, I will satisfy every desire, even the desires of your heart you do not realize are there. Make a vow to stay.

Kellie: *I love You, Lord, and I Love Your presence. I'll do what is required to show up at the table ready to hear what You are saying to me. I enjoy being with You in spite of myself and my mess.*

Lord, I give You...

❝ I will be found. ❞

Jesus says to me...

❝ I can't enjoy your presence without you.... ❞

Jesus, I want You to know...

Processing His Word in His Presence

Revelation 1:1-18

Revelation 3:20

Matthew 11:25-30

ENCOUNTER 1: I AM AWAKENED

Encounter 2

Jesus explained, "I am the Way, I am the Truth, and I am the Life. No one comes next to the Father except through union with me. To know me is to know my Father too. And from now on you will realize that you have seen him and experienced him."

John 14:6-7 (TPT)

AN INVITATION TO THE THRONE ROOM

> Make it stop. You're blaming others for your situation. You continue to gaze at your hurt, fatigue and lack. You worry that others won't see you, believe in you and support you. You listen to the lies of the enemy more than you hear My truth about you. You wrestle against flesh and blood, against the temporary things.

Kellie: *I repent, my Jesus. I turn my gaze on You. I listen to You only!*

Jesus, I...

"None of that matters to My plan. None of it should stop you from *becoming* what I have called you. For I am coming soon, swiftly and all at once, sweeping people into the Kingdom. I have chosen you, this place, your family as a resting place, a clearinghouse for My glory.

This house is My house, so let go of your fears and concerns. Let go of your past. Take upon yourself *My* past, *My* sacrifice, *My* blood, *My* body, My freedom, *My* yoke.

My yoke is to love the Lord your God, our Father, without any concern for Myself. Learn of Me. I'll teach you and school you in the ways to love Him fully and wholeheartedly. I'll teach you to come to Him intimately."

Kellie: *Teach me, Lord Jesus.*

Jesus, I want to learn of You. Sometimes I feel like...

Jesus says to me...

> I am the doorway to the Father. I will escort you into His presence with singing. In worship, you will enter the throne room. You've only practiced this so far, but see now: the gates of Heaven are open wide. Heaven is not only bursting out toward you, Heaven is inviting you in.

My Jesus, I want You to know...

Processing His Word in His Presence

John 14

Romans 5:1-2

John 15:14-17 TPT

Encounter 3

So now we draw near freely and boldly to where grace is enthroned, to receive mercy's kiss and discover the grace we urgently need to strengthen us in our time of weakness.

Hebrews 4:16 (TPT)

THINGS TO COME

> You will be escorted by Me into the throne room in these coming days. There, you will receive many things you need to complete your assignment. You'll know the love of your Father. You'll know His grace for you, for mankind. You'll be filled with all the knowledge and the weight of your glory.

Kellie: *"My" glory, Lord?*

> You have come short of the Father's glory, but you are walking into the fullness as you join your life fully with Mine. This is not your glory because it originates with you, but I call it "your glory" because it belongs to you! Our glory is YOUR glory, and by original design, a divine human right.

Lord, this makes me think...

❝ I will guide and usher you in these things. The protocol of the throne room is always one of love. Love first! You will see evidence of how much We love you everywhere. You cannot escape it. The Father will fill you with His love. Then, there will be times from that place, at the moment I release you, when you will be able to make your requests known.

We already know what you need, but the process of your coming and your asking is a joy to us. It's like a celebration to be able to give you whatever you ask!

You've thought it difficult to receive from the Father, but it is not! Many times, you've asked amiss, but you were learning and developing in My ways. Up until now, you have remained in My outer courts, all the while coming closer into My presence. As you draw nearer to Me and know Me more intimately, I will draw you into the Father's presence. Will you take My hand? ❞

Jesus, I...

> "I've been waiting for this time to come! I am preparing you for The Day! At this point in the throne room, you'll be granted what you have asked. By the time you come to this place, the sin that drives you to ask amiss has been exposed and burned in My fire. Old things are gone and what's left is of Me."

Kellie: *Lord, I want this! I want You! I lay down in Your beautiful presence. Cleanse me from anything that keeps me from intimacy with You.*

Lord, I want...

Jesus says to me...

Processing His Word in His Presence

Ephesians 3

Ephesians 4:4-9, 11-13, 18-20

James 4:1-10

Encounter 4

The Sovereign LORD has given me a well-instructed tongue, to know the word that sustains the weary. He wakens me morning by morning, wakens my ear to listen like one being instructed.

Isaiah 50:4 (NIV)

GOOD MORNING

> Good morning! You say 'good morning' lightly, as a greeting starting a conversation. When I say 'good morning,' I am blessing you with the goodness of the Father and pouring in to your day. I am giving you the will to have a good morning and the power to press into My grace by faith. When you put faith in My words, the grace is the power to bring it into manifestation. How about that for a good morning!

Kellie: *I receive the blessing of a good morning! Good morning to You too! What would make this a good morning for You? I am Yours today.*

Good morning, Lord...

Jesus says to me...

> These individual sacrifices of your life mean more than you know. One good morning turns into a day, then turns into a week and into a month. These times together will grow increasingly frequent as we develop day by day to the place where we will speak, act and move as One.

Lord Jesus, I...

> There are plans and purposes stirring in your heart already that are beginning to burn. It doesn't seem to you that you have the ability, finances, understanding or connections to accomplish them. Yet, you *already* are connected! I am the connection who will bring ability, finances, and understanding. Don't allow the enemy to shame you for weakness in any area. For your weakness is My open door when you realize that I never meant you to succeed in anything without Me. Your significance in these days is great, yet the perfection of your calling is not on you—but on Me. And I glory in that assignment for I have already paid the price for this fellowship. As you simply yield your time and affection, our times together will be the empowerment you need.

Jesus says to me...

Lord, I'm realizing that...

"There will be precious days to come when you are summoned once again to the throne room. These times are special to Me for I yearn to come before the Father as one with you. As you leave the throne room, you will have what you need to do your assignment. You'll know your place, your plan and your instructions. You'll know you are supplied for every detail.

My grace that allows you this entrance is all that you need as you place your confidence and hope in Me. Your times and your call is of Me—not of man. I've prepared you for this journey into the discovery of who you are."

Jesus says to me...

"You've desired to know the mysteries (Matthew 13:11-12, 16-17), but you didn't know what it would look like. It is different than you thought. It was a mystery! But it is being *revealed*. I am being revealed, unveiled right before your eyes. Yes eyes, for you'll see many things in the coming days that will be like Heaven on earth."

Lord, I open my eyes to see...

Processing His Word in His Presence

Hebrews 4 TPT

Psalm 31:15 NLT

Romans 11:29

Matthew 13:9-12

Encounter 5

*The eyes of the Lord are upon even the
weakest worshipers who love him—
those who wait in hope and expectation
for the strong, steady love of God.*

Psalm 33:18 (TPT)

WAIT FOR ME

> **What are your concerns today? Can I have them? There isn't a lot I can do until you let Me have your cares. See if I will not trade your cares for My peace and rest. And answers! I have answers for every difficulty you face. Have you asked Me to help you?**

Lord Jesus, I have to admit that I...

> I have noticed that many times when you pray about the issues that weigh on your heart, we don't communicate as well as we could. Let's repair what keeps you from receiving My help. Think of your greatest care. Have you asked Me for help and expected My help by faith? Have you asked Me to actually help **you** or have you been asking Me to change what others are doing that bothers you? I am here to help **you**. Ask Me. What do you need? Make your requests and wants known to Me! It is My joy to help you.

My greatest care is...

_____
_____
_____
_____
_____

I'm also concerned about...

_____
_____
_____
_____
_____

❝Wait! When you pray, when you ask for help—wisdom, mercy, or anything—don't ask and move on. Don't have the last word when you pray. Let Me respond! I have answers. I have correction, encouragement and, particularly, I have promises to make to you. When you receive My words, faith is born in your heart. This is faith to move, faith to win. As you continue to listen to Me, I will give you word after word. Faith is authored and continually developed in My presence. When doubt, fear, rejection or shame come, bring them to Me. I will give you a faith injection every time! Don't come to Me in your strength, but come to Me *for My strength*. I will give you rest. Now, ask Me again. Then, incline your ear to hear from Me.❞

You're right, Jesus. I ask for Your help with...

Jesus says to me...

"Now, go in peace and safety today. Let Me be your confidence as you walk through your day. Your plate of care is empty! Your day is carefree! Be constantly aware that I am fulfilling My promise to you to care *for* you. See what it's like to live and move in *My* strength today. Be sensitive to My leading, and you will see through My eyes. Every situation you encounter will be seen through the eyes of faith, love, mercy and plenty. I don't view life through fear, hate, self-centeredness or scarcity, and neither will you. *This* is the day that I have made, and you will rejoice and be glad in it!"

Yes, Lord! I receive today as a gift from You, and I will...

Processing His Word in His Presence

1 Peter 5:7 AMP

Isaiah 50:31

Hebrews 12:1-3 NIV

2 Corinthians 12:10

Encounter 6

For in him we live and move and exist. As some of your own poets have said, "We are his offspring."

Acts 17:28 (NLT)

BE ON ASSIGNMENT

*"*You have an assignment for the Kingdom! You are to spread freedom, love, acceptance and fire to My precious people today. Don't be afraid to step out for I have called you by My name.

Take ground for My Kingdom as you bring Me to the people you encounter. As you remain aware of My presence, you can expose people to My love even in passing.

If I call your attention to a particular soul, you will have courage and knowledge. You will be filled with the courage to be bold and reach out. You will be given knowledge to reach that one I show you for My glory. This day is of Me and My making, and it will be blessed. It will flourish and be filled with miracles. Expect Me to move wherever you go. In everything you do today, in all you set your hands to, be aware of My purpose in it.

When you live your life unto Me, as your daily sacrifice, a simple hug becomes My divine life flow. My fire will be imparted when I give you words to speak. Will you do this for Me?*"*

Lord Jesus, I...

Jesus says to me...

" Your love allows Me to reach others, and I am pleased by that and grateful to you. I am doing some things for you that you will like! As you walk in unified presence with Me, you'll not fall short and you'll not diminish.

Trust Me to open doors for you. That is not your job but mine. I will lead you and usher you daily in every step. I have a plan. You're right where I want you to be and doing fine. I'm correcting what needs correcting for I know your heart. I am repairing and reworking your finances, family, life, work and household as we walk together. "

I love You, Jesus, and ...

> Begin to say with confidence: 'As for me and my house, we will serve the Lord.' Your house is My house. Never forget this. You are a fine steward, and I am the divine supply. As you do what I tell you, miracles will happen. Whatever I say to you, no matter how big it sounds, don't think it can't be done. Just make the first move in faith, and I will take it from there. One action at a time, winning and victorious, we overcome the world.

Jesus, when You tell me I'm a fine steward, I feel like...

Jesus says to me...

Processing His Word in His Presence

Matthew 6:19-24

Deuteronomy 30:20

Acts 17:24-29

Encounter 7

You live fully in me and now I live fully in them so that they will experience perfect unity, and the world will be convinced that you have sent me, for they will see that you love each one of them with the same passionate love that you have for me.

John 17:23 (TPT)

MY HOUSE

"I'm coming close! I'm closer even now, easing My life into your soul. I've come to bring salvation to the hurting and deceved places. I'm coming first to My household. I will set in order everything in My house so that I might have a place fit to bring My lost ones and guests home. I will have a house where we can celebrate My love for you and others. It will be a place to call home where I can rest My Spirit, My Glory and My love."

Lord, when You say hurting and deceived places, I think about...

"My presence will dwell in My house like an overflowing fountain. *You* are My house. I will first make My home in your heart, your mind, your will and your emotions. I will walk with you through the hurts, troubles and weaknesses that have long caused you trouble. I will walk you through the minefield of hidden places of destruction, exposing what has prevented you from manifested glory.

As you cast these burdens on Me, I will burn to ash every enemy that has gathered in your soul, and you will begin to rise up as you become one with My strength. In My presence, you are changed, the first fruit of My burning, purifying fire coming to humanity. Will you walk with Me? Sit with Me through this judgment of sin and everything that causes sin."

Lord, as You walk through my heart, I am listening because I want to be free from...

❝ Does this cause you concern? Think with Me about the things you've held on to. I will bring some to your mind now. Don't be afraid to be transparent with Me. Don't be afraid I will turn you away as you reveal your heart to Me. Be still and know that I am God. Be still and let Me heal you. ❞

Jesus says to me...

Jesus, I give You...

> There will be no stone, no hidden reef or hard place left in you when we are done. This finishing work I am bringing to My people will be the finished work of the cross and resurrection. I will have the fullness of what I gave My life to win, a body fitly joined together and a Church without spot or wrinkle. I will have My House prepared for the harvest from which My glory will flow. This is the awakening, this is the end-time sweeping.
>
> Together, we will harvest the hurting, the blind, the broken—all who will come. And they will come. They will not be able to resist My love coming out of you. My love for the world will be seen, and they will come to My saving grace.
>
> The world and the kingdoms of the world will bow their knee, not because they have to in defeat, but in worship, declaring *Jesus is Lord!*
>
> That's why I'm knocking. Thank you for answering.

Thank You, Lord, for...

Encounter 8

*Be still, and know that I am God! I
will be honored by every nation. I will
be honored throughout the world.*

Psalm 46:10 (NLT)

Jesus says to me...

Processing His Word in His Presence

Luke 15:1-7

Jude 1:17-23

Matthew 13:24-30

Luke 3:16-17

COME IN

"My Father has called you to come to Me. Come into a new depth of My Presence. You're home now, not lost, not abandoned and not rejected.

Come into the stillness where you will begin to know that I am God. It is My desire for your heart to understand that you are not forgotten. Even as you spend purposeful time with Me, My words will drive out the lies of the enemy and replace them with My truth. Correcting the thought processes in your heart will bring changes in your life—not only in ways you've asked for but also in ways you didn't know you needed."

Lord, what lie am I believing about...

Jesus says to me...

❝ Stop being hard on yourself. I see and know every crevice of your soul. As I am allowed to recreate your mind, will and emotions, you will no longer be limited to what you know. You will not be limited to your ability to work. I will be working things out on your behalf. Oh, the great plans I have laid out for you. Although you cannot conceive it now, greatness is in you, waiting to be revealed. I have created you to thrive, prosper and impact others. You soon will see this! ❞

Jesus, You say greatness is in me, but I have felt limited by...

_____

_____

_____

_____

_____

_____

Jesus says to me...

_____

_____

_____

_____

_____

_____

" I will begin to build deep understanding with My words of power and blessing. My words are life to you. The words I have given you in your Bible and those I am now pouring into you. Take them seriously and take them to your heart. Words that carry grace, healing and power for change are always flowing from Heaven to you.

The most precious offering to Me, is an ear to hear and a desire to understand. Trust is built on relationship and relationship on experience. I never meant My words to be merely read in a book. They are meant to be heard in your heart. I don't know you as merely one *among* many but as an individual, as one *of* many. I designed you to know Me as I know you, and here you are, fellowshipping with Me and connecting with My plan and power. "

I'm ready to hear Your words, Jesus. I trust You....

> My resurrection power is in you in abundance. You know this as a 'promise,' but I want you to know it by experiencing Me—resurrected *life* Himself, converging with the realities of your day!
>
> Today's victory begins with My explosive words. It seems too simple. And yet, by My words the worlds were framed, and you were created. I spoke you into existence, and I have not stopped speaking to you, of you or for you. I have mentioned you to My Father many times. Our heart is for you. Our plan is to bring you to a place of complete wholeness. Don't worry over how things have been up until now. You have not been far away from My plan at any time. I have created you for a Kingdom purpose. You are called, anointed, strengthened and supplied in this time and for this moment. You will not fail or come short.

Jesus says to me...

_____

_____

_____

_____

_____

Processing His Word in His Presence

John 6:35-40

Acts 17:22-30

Isaiah 55

Encounter 9

When you release Your Spirit-Wind, life is created, ready to replenish life upon the earth.

Psalm 104:30 (TPT)

GRACE AND FAVOR

Kellie: *Hover over the waters of my heart, Lord Jesus!*

"My heart for you is full of love and compassion. I am moving in this day to bring relief to your life. Raise your expectations today! Lay hold in the Spirit for the kind of day I want you to experience.

Impact, joy, productivity, peace, favor, prosperity and love—these are the powers I have called you to walk in. Filling your day with *grace* is what I want to do. Grace is not simply mercy for failures but *My* power on you to do what you cannot do.

With My grace, there is no reason for stress or care. Let Me make your way. Expect My favor to give you favor with others. When I put words in your mouth, you can expect others to hear you. When I tell you what to do, expect the situation will work out for your good as you follow Me. I will move with you in this way if you will expect Me to. I have the plan, and I will give it to you. And you will like it."

I want You to move in my life today, Lord! I expect...

Jesus says to me...

> As you work on My behalf, I am working on yours. It will not be long until you'll see the manifestation of My plan, My glory and My resurrection life flood your soul, life, body and family. Receive it by faith today as you would if your birthday were coming. My relief is coming. My Help is here. The changes you'll see in your life will be better than any birthday gift.
>
> Expect clarity of My voice and direction. Expect ease in hearing and expect My words to flow. Remember, I have provisioned you for all I have called you to do. Stop acting as though you do these things on your own. I've called you by name. I've given you an assignment. My Spirit will flow through you, gracing you to succeed.

Jesus says to me...

Lord Jesus, I receive Your grace on me to...

> **I have many wonder-filled things to show you. Here begins what you will call the best days of your life.**

Jesus says to me...

Processing His Word in His Presence

Hebrews 3

Psalm 104

James 1

Encounter 10

And all of us, as with unveiled face… continued to behold [in the Word of God] as in a mirror the glory of the Lord, are constantly being transfigured into His very own image in ever increasing splendor and from one degree of glory to another; [for this comes] from the Lord [Who is] the Spirit.

2 Corinthians 3:18 (AMPC)

FACE TO FACE

"I'm opening My Word to you so you can see My heart of love and grace. I don't see your broken life. When I look in you, I see Me. Look in the mirror by looking in the Word to see Me.

Keep looking with a steady, unwavering gaze. Don't look away! This is transformational face-to-face living. Face to face *is* looking in the mirror. Look into Me for I am looking into you."

Jesus, I want to say...

> I know every part of you. Your eyes are the window to your soul. Keep looking at Me so I can flood your heart with My healing, cleansing and purifying *light!* Darkness is destroyed as I show you unrighteousness—anything not right or out of order that needs fixing. I show you these things not so you will feel shame or remorse but so you will be enabled to repent and go free, for as we gaze face to face, you are literally changed into My image.

Jesus, shine light in my heart. I feel like...

Jesus says to me...

❝ There is *nothing* that can keep Me from looking at you and pouring My life into you. Let *nothing* keep you from looking at Me. Don't attempt to rid yourself of unrighteousness or imperfection before coming to Me. You cannot do it. You were not designed to save yourself. That's My part! Your part is to simply come to Me as you are with a humble heart, pouring yourself out and into Me complete with your strengths *and* weaknesses.

Life with Me is *not* hard. It's the pretense of life with Me that is difficult. Let it go! I'll show you the way. **❞**

Kellie: *Am I hiding shame?*

Jesus, I need You to save me from...

> I've been waiting a long time for you to know Me as I have known you. I've been waiting to walk as One with you, going from one degree of glory to the next. Doing Our Father's will and defeating the enemy is what We were born for, you and I. Are you as eager and excited as I am? If you knew My plans for Our victory, you would be excited too! Come. I'm ready to show you! Just look in the mirror of My Word.

I am ready to see You face to face, Jesus...

Jesus says to me...

Processing His Word in His Presence

2 Corinthians 3, 4

1 John 1

1 Corinthians 13:9-13

Encounter 11

Jesus said to her, "You don't have to wait any longer, the Anointed One is here speaking with you—I am the One you're looking for."

John 4:26 (TPT)

THIS IS ME

Kellie: *I worship You, Jesus. I give You my life, my essence, my all. You are in the process of coming, and You're closer than You've ever been. You are my Jesus, the beginning and the end.*

You hold me firmly in Your hand today. Thank You for leading me, giving me Your thoughts and words to say. I belong to You and no other.

Jesus, I worship You. I give You...

> "I am coming. I've been coming for thousands of years. My glory, which is My presence, is filling the earth and soon to break forth and overflow. You will be in the middle of it.
>
> Yes, this is Me talking to you—My words flowing through to your heart. It is My desire to have free and open two-way communication with you. You are My joy, yet you don't even know how much I love and care for you."

Jesus says to me…

When I hear this, I feel like…

Jesus says to me...

Lord, I want to say...

> When I met the woman at the well, it was this type of communication that showed her the reality and depth of My love and opened the door for her to receive My cleansing truth.
>
> Cleansing truth is like having your house professionally deep-cleaned for you—so fresh and pleasant and functional. You don't have to keep the door closed to guests. So it is with your soul. I am knocking on the door of your heart. Yes, throw open your doors to Me. For I am coming. I have been coming and will be coming.

Kellie: *Come, Lord Jesus, come! Make me ready for Your glory.*

I want Your cleansing truth, Lord Jesus. Come! Make me...

Jesus says to me...

Processing His Word in His Presence

John 4:1-42

John 10:1-21

Revelation 1:12-19

Encounter 12

...Those who set their gaze deeply into the perfecting law of liberty are fascinated by and respond to the truth they hear and are strengthened by it—they experience God's blessing in all that they do!

James 1:25 (TPT)

GAZE DEEPLY

"My face is always toward you! I am giving you answers moment by moment, and I am always aware of what is going on in your heart and mind. I am moving you to the ultimate awareness of knowing what is going on in *My* heart and mind.

As you walk with Me and allow Me to take the lead, your trust in Me will increase a hundredfold. Even beyond the increase, the impact of it will multiply over and over. This is your overflowing cup. Though it may seem messy at times, you will be consistently full of My presence. When it doesn't feel like it, turn back to face Me, and you will find Me."

I turn my face to You, Jesus, and I see…

> "Your growing faith in Me is pleasing, but you continue to strive to accomplish change on your own—change in yourself, circumstances, lifestyle and others. Stop the struggle to change! Instead, focus your labor on resting in Me. Your trust allows Me full range to move on your behalf, unhindered by your shortcomings or fears."

Kellie: *Jesus, what am I afraid of?*

Jesus says to me...

> "'I am the Way' to change anything and everything! You want Me to tell you to 'do' something to bring change, but fear is rebuked by simply resting in Me and in My Words. Can you?

Lord Jesus, I...

> "You've made progress, but we are not done. We have much more cleansing left to see to. Check your heart now. Did the thought of that bring comfort or hurt to your soul?"

Jesus, I feel…

❝ Thank you for coming to Me and letting Me know how you feel. I want you to feel. I made you to feel. If you refuse to feel a problem, you won't deal with it. I want more for you! These misunderstandings and lack of understanding about the heart and mind lead not only to shame and hurt remaining undetected but they also dull you to the full experience of My love and approval of you.

The enemy is full of deceit and tries to convince you to hide from My face in shame. We will catch him at his tricks. Allow no thought to stand except My love, manifested in correction and in My best *life* ahead for you.

This is the face-to-face life! ❞

Jesus says to me...

" As you grow up in Me in the coming weeks and months, don't allow your attention to focus on how others lead their lives or respond to your transformation. Don't judge—just respond in My love. Literally, you have My Love to love with. Rest in that love not only for yourself but also for them.

I am doing a work in the hearts of others that you are not aware of. So, remain in Me. You know My love intimately, and I am manifesting My love to them now. How powerful it is when you allow Me to love others through you, to back up and affirm My quiet love spoken in their hearts. You are a partaker and a partner with the heavenly calling! "

Lord, You are...

Jesus says to me...

> "Follow My leading in your words and actions. I will prove Myself to you. I will show you My glory."

Kellie: *Yes, to all of it, Jesus! I am Your servant! I am Yours! I declare that I will experience the greatest joy there is! Your perfection is released into every part of my being! There is nothing missing and nothing broken in my life. You overwhelm my failures with Your generous grace.*

Jesus, I declare that I...

_____

_____

_____

_____

Jesus says to me...

_____

_____

_____

Processing His Word in His Presence

Hebrews 4

Ephesians 3:14-21

James 1:25-26

Encounter 13

The Spirit and the bride say, "Come." Let anyone who hears this say, "Come." Let anyone who is thirsty come. Let anyone who desires drink freely from the water of life.

Revelation 22:17 (NLT)

OUR JOY

Kellie: *I love You, Jesus, and I love Your name. I love being called by Your name and called to Your presence. You have said to me, "I am coming." Well, Lord, I say to You, I am coming!*

Lord Jesus, I say to You...

> **Making time for Me is a life-altering priority. The things I want to do in you are vast and wonderful. You don't know the half of it. Trust Me when I say, 'You'll like it!' We have so very much to accomplish and so little time. Bring yourself to Me with an eager heart, and We will make quick progress.**

Lord, my heart is...

Jesus says to me...

> I have called you by name, created you for My greatness and to show forth My glory. We will open the eyes of people to My saving love and grace. You were designed to offer My love to people—hurting people who don't know why they're hurting or those who refuse to see that they are hurting. They've wandered from My love and don't even know it! Your time with Me today will alter not only your life but also those you come in contact with. You are My joy carrier.

Lord, this makes me...

> To bring a smile to someone's face and bubbling joy into a life is My very joyful assignment.

Imagine how I feel as My people are freed from chains, lies, sin and heartache. I'm thrilled! The moments I have with you when you allow Me to work in your life give Me the satisfaction and joy of shepherding you. Even so, I receive even greater enjoyment working *with you* to bring this freedom to those I place in your path.

Jesus says to me...

Kellie: *Thank You, Jesus, for what You're doing in us! How can we make Your day today? That's an open question to You. We want to bring this joy to those around us. Show us Your joy! Show us Your glory!*

Yes, Lord! Show me...

Jesus says to me...

Processing His Word in His Presence

Revelation 22:17

Romans 12:1-2

1 John 1:1-4

Encounter 14

Now hope does not disappoint, because the love of God has been poured out in our hearts by the Holy Spirit who was given to us.

Romans 5:5 (NKJV)

PERFECT LOVE

"Remember this truth today: You are full of My love. Don't see it as a pot that is merely filled up and full but a pot filled with a flow that doesn't stop. You are a container that is full to overflowing because My Love doesn't stop flowing when it's used or poured out. The first purpose of the love of God is to fill your being with Our love. I came as the Father's Messenger, carrying His perfect love to be poured out to and through you. Meditate on that today!

Sometimes it is difficult to love others. Out of obedience to My Word and the Father's commandment, you have exerted effort to make yourself love anyway. I am honored by your obedience, but I am also showing you a better way. Allow My love—Father's love—to saturate your being. Regardless of circumstances, choose to believe We have this great love for you. Do not allow shame, hurt, rejection or disappointment to filter or diminish the flow of Our love as it fills you up today."

Kellie: *Lord, I choose now to believe that You—Father, Spirit and Son—love me unconditionally and fully. I receive Your care for me and for all that concerns me. Open my eyes to what this means and how this changes my life.*

Jesus, I choose...

> Now you are positioned for My Love to flow through you no matter how difficult the situation around you is. You no longer need to struggle to love, for I will birth and renew in you a love for others. You overflow the very love that sent Me to the cross to pay the price for those who despised and abandoned Me. Remember, when it's hard to love, stop and meditate. I will show you how to connect to My love every time. Still your thoughts, close your eyes and say this to Me: 'I love You, Jesus.' Listen for My response afterward.

I love You, Jesus!

Jesus says to me...

> "I will always respond. Trust Me to speak so that you can hear Me. Trust yourself to hear. You were made to hear My voice. Many times you hear Me, but you don't trust yourself to believe it's Me. Let Me teach you to know My voice. When you hear Me speak the words, 'I love you,' the very words contain the power to cast out fear, worry, anger and sin. I want to fill you with rhema words—freshly spoken words from Heaven."

Jesus, I trust You to...

Jesus says to me...

❝ Get ready, My love. For when you receive what I am giving you, it will be the freest life you can live. For you to be able, quick and disposed and to love without concern or thought for yourself will set you free. It won't matter to you what someone else does. Neither your future, your joy, nor your life is connected to anyone else's love or favor. ❞

Lord Jesus, I...

> My love alive in you is what lets you know I am your Savior, King, Provider and Source. That same love will love others well. I've designed the days ahead to highlight My love in you. Yes, it will be a gift to others, but I want it first to be a gift to you. I love you first, then you love others best. You'll see and revel in the difference My love makes.

Kellie: *Lord Jesus, I dedicate and give You my soul today. My mind, will and emotions are Yours to fill, use, mold and lead. Take my life to another level in Your love today. I will listen and hear You speak Your love to me today and from now on. I will take You at Your Word, in Jesus' name! Thank You for always meeting me, always speaking and always loving me! I love You, Jesus.*

And I also love You, Jesus. Take my life and...

Jesus says to me...

> **And I love you too!**

Processing His Word in His Presence

Romans 5:1-11

1 John 3:18-23

1 John 4:7-18

ENCOUNTER 14: PERFECT LOVE

Encounter 15

The Father of life sent me, and he is my life. In the same way, the one who feeds upon me, I will become his life.

John 6:57 (TPT)

TAKE AND EAT COMMUNION

> Healing and miracles are the children's bread, like manna from Heaven to keep My loved ones healthy, strong and free from the curse of pain and disease. I have redeemed you from everything that is under the curse of the law. So, eat of Me, take Me in fully. Allow Me to permeate your soul *and* body.

Kellie: *Lord Jesus, Healer and Savior, I want my vessel to be clean and pure for Your service. You are so good and gracious to Your people and merciful to those who look to You for help. I want to be so full of You—less of me, more of You.*

My Jesus, Healer and Savior, I want...

> "I want to fill you to overflowing. I am enlarging your capacity—spirit, soul and body. We are making room in your heart for more of Me."

Jesus says to me...

> "I'm doing My work in you. I know that at times it hurts, but you'll be so glad when all the junk is cleaned out and removed from your heart. There is a capacity for power there that will astound you, but the experience you will like even more is receiving the joy of My presence. I know because, as a Man, I experience this same joy when I am in My Father's presence.
>
> I am the Door for you to come into His presence. We both belong there. I love to worship Him, and when you worship Him, We come into His presence together. Be more aware of this truth, for it's a miracle."

Have Your way, Lord. I worship You, my King...

> **"** Don't rely on corporate worship. When your objective is true worship, you bring Me to the corporate worship. Corporate worship is powerful when all have their faces pointed toward the Father. Look in My face, for you'll find Him there. When you gaze at Me, you'll see His heart toward you—full of love, healing, provision, belonging, restoration, *life*. **"**

Look at Me! What do you see?

When I look at You, I see...

"Receive what is pouring out by the Holy Spirit from the Father to you. This is your daily bread, take and eat. We are united with your spirit, soul and *body!* This is the miracle manifestation I walked in while I was in the earth, and now, I walk the earth in you. There is bread in My house, My dwelling place. Don't allow your heart to be too hard or distracted to take Me in as the healer and the giver of life, your sustaining force, your bread. Likewise, don't harden your heart to *your* part of this serving of bread. This is the bread, and My presence is the wine I wanted Martha to eat and serve. Martha's heart was hardened by care and, though it was what I wanted for her, she did not eat. The eating and drinking was done by Mary. Will you eat?"

Lord Jesus, I celebrate You today and take and eat of Your body. I remember Your love for me today as I worship You and receive every part of the redemptive work You purchased for me (1 Corinthians 11:24-29). Thank You, Jesus, for...

Jesus says to me...

Thank You, precious Savior, for healing and restoring me. I will continue eating Your words and drinking of Your presence. I am so grateful. Have Your way in me today!

Processing His Word in His Presence

Matthew 15:21-28

Deuteronomy 28:58-63

Galatians 3:1-14

John 6:22-58

Encounter 16

When the Spirit of truth comes, he will guide you into all truth. He will not speak on his own but will tell you what he has heard. He will tell you about the future.

John 16:13 (NLT)

DAYS OF HEAVEN

"I am pouring Myself out fully in these days. I could not pour out the full revelation of Myself to the disciples in John 16, but when the Holy Spirit was poured out, He began to bring revelation of all that is to come. Little by little, the Father's message has been brought to the hungry, and the revelation of the sons and daughters of God is now at hand."

Jesus says to me...

> **The days of the fullness of My Spirit—My full anointing and power dwelling in My body—have arrived. Since the Day of Pentecost, My Spirit has been filling you, purifying you, preparing you and revealing Myself to you that you might reveal My glory in the earth. This is that which was spoken by the prophet Joel, spoken of in Acts and promised by Me when I said, 'He will tell you the future.'**

Lord Jesus, it seems like...

Jesus says to me...

❝ This is the revealing. See the open door? I am calling you to unify your heart with Mine by the Holy Spirit. I take from the Father and give it to the Spirit to pour out to you, the life-altering words of His truth. You must simply receive and believe His words in order to be changed.

As My Word fills you and your worship pours forth, you will live in Our presence. We will live in power in and through you to bring Our Father's good plan to His children. We will do great things—greater than have ever been seen on the earth before. I am making you into My image. You are coming alive! ❞

Jesus, I have to say...

> Like Sleeping Beauty, you are waking up into a new life and a new day. Realize it's a new day for Me too, for I have waited for this day since before creation. My Father has been patient for His children to come to Him, but He has grown eager and excited about the days ahead. He is on the edge of His seat, ready for you and I to live and move as One with Him. Living every day in His presence, we will finally see the great harvest of people come running into the Kingdom because His glorified Church will shine with My light and love.

Jesus says to me...

"Welcome to the future!"

Thank You, Jesus! You are...

Processing His Word in His Presence

John 14-16

Joel 2:28-29

Acts 2:16-21

Encounter 17

But those who set their gaze deeply into the perfecting law of liberty are fascinated by and respond to the truth they hear and are strengthened by it—they experience God's blessing in all that they do!

James 1:25 (TPT)

A NEW DAY

> 'Show me Your glory, Lord,' you have said. You wanted this, so now expect it! Daily, My goodness is coming toward you with all the power and life which emanates from Me. That force is love. My love for you flows to you—to you and through you.

Jesus says to me...

Lord, You know my heart! I want...

> Restoration is coming. Very soon, you'll see this miracle begin. Let it be a sign to you of My loving goodness and My faithfulness flowing to you. Let it be a sign to you that your sins and your past are forgiven. Nothing of your making will stop or delay what is of Me.

Lord Jesus, that's a big promise! Help me to...

Jesus says to me...

> The turnaround of your life and your house will be a wonder to you and a sign of My love. Your house will be transformed into a shepherd's house. One of My greatest needs on the earth today is a physical and tangible place where people can come to meet Me. This is revival! In revival, My body will be filled with My presence and soaked with worship. If you continue to behold Me, speak of Me and learn of Me and not look for man's recognition or validation, I will use your life to show forth My presence, My Love and My saving power to the world. They will look at you, but they will see Me, the *I AM*. They will be glad for they will know I have come to save them.

Jesus, I worship You...

❝ Have peace about your loved ones and use your words in partnership with Me. I'll give you the words I want you to say. You will enjoy the next season even in challenging situations. As you walk with Me, you'll begin to see the fruit of abiding increase in you and around you. Be full of My joy today. My favor and My Father's favor go before you. Rest in My Word and My Love for you, casting all your cares into My hands. This is your armor and your strength. ❞

Jesus, thank You. I bring my loved ones to You today...

Jesus says to me...

Processing His Word in His Presence

Isaiah 43:19

1 Peter 5:1-7 TPT

Luke 15:1-7

Encounter 18

See, I have engraved you on the palms of my hands; your walls are ever before me.

Isaiah 49:16 (NIV)

LIVING *IN* ME

> "Separate yourself from your own reputation and self-promotion. I'm in charge of that and you trust Me, so let it go. Let Me and your awareness of Me grow in you. You can't look to others as your life source and grow more full of Me at the same time. It must be more of Me, less of you."

Lord, to me that means...

Jesus says to me...

> "This is how I am with My Father so I fully contain Him. You will contain this treasure as you fill up on Me! Fill up with more, more and more of the glory until it spills out your face and shines like a burning light. This has always been My plan. It's thrilling to Me to be at this time and place of unveiling and sharing revelation with you. Press, press, press into Me. Don't relent! Like an empty cup submerged, you will quickly come up full of glory, spilling over with healing power, miracles and love. You are a vital part of the greater works I spoke of coming to pass. My hand is on you. My body has all fallen short of My glory *thus far,* but open your heart to the picture of a glorified Church, without spot or wrinkle. You will *not* fall short of all that My Father has decreed. His will be done in Heaven and on the earth. *You* can decree this with Me, and We will walk in it together."

Kellie: *Oh Lord, I receive it! I lay down my life before You and soak in Your Presence. I receive Your Words. In my stillness, I receive You.*

I lay down everything in worship and soak in Your presence. In the stillness, I...

Jesus says to me...

> "'In the name of Jesus' is not what you say to speak in authority because I am *not* with you. It is what you say to declare your authority because *I am* with you! I am not only in you, *you* are *in Me*. The name of Jesus is a strong tower because it is Me. Stop and meditate on this distinct reality."

Kellie: *Lord, I see it! In You I live and move and have my being… (Acts 17:28). I am literally in You, in Your name! In You, in Your name, I am free, healed, restored physically, debt-free, trauma-free, spirit, soul and body! I go free, and I go! I am about my Savior's business! In Jesus' name, I throw off these old grave clothes! In Jesus' name, I am clothed in righteousness, peace and joy in the Holy Ghost! I have all that I need. I shall not want. You have made me to lie down in green pastures. You have restored my soul. When I walk through the valley of the shadow of death, I have no fear. For You are with me. I am in You. Your protection and correction give me comfort, for You keep me in You. I do not go astray for I am in the palm of Your hand. You lead me through to still waters and guide me down the right path as I walk in Your name. You honor me to sit with You. You anoint my head and heal me in the presence of my enemies. I am hidden yet glorified in You, and my cup overflows today. Your goodness and unfailing love run after me every day. I will live with You forever, for I will never leave and You will never leave me!*

Lord Jesus, this means that...

Jesus says to me...

I declare in the name of Jesus...

Processing His Word in His Presence

John 14:1-14

Romans 15:1-14

2 Corinthians 4:7

Psalm 23

Encounter 19

...*"My Father! If it is possible, let this cup of suffering be taken away from me. Yet I want your will to be done, not mine."*

Matthew 26:39 (NLT)

LOOK TO ME

"Making Me the center is making Me powerful in your life, to the point of My manifested glory. I overcame My greatest challenge in the garden of Gethsemane by making My Father the center of My mind, will and emotions. I set My face like flint on Him, My words establishing My heart and soul: 'My Father! If it is possible, let this cup of suffering be taken away from Me. Yet I want Your will to be done, not Mine.'

If I had yielded to My own desire, it would not have taken Me to My destiny, nor seated Me at My Father's side. The pain of Hell and death paled in comparison to resurrection glory. What you see around you now will be inconsequential as the coming glory is revealed."

I want to see Your glory...

Jesus says to me...

> Do as I did. Direct your face and attention on the glory and the light that shines from My face. This is joy—the entrance of joy. The highway by which joy travels. Joy is simply My presence flowing to you by way of your attention. It flows into your present circumstances, strengthening and delivering you from all destruction and pain. You lift your eyes, and I will lift your soul.

That sounds too easy, Jesus. But I lift my eyes to You, and I open my soul...

> Fear is the killer distraction. This is why I say repeatedly, 'Fear not!' Recognize fear in its hiding places and disguises. I will uncover it as I did for My disciples. As My humble disciple, you will repent, resist and rebuke what I reveal. I am teaching and training you, and I will have the companionship with you that My heart desires.

Jesus says to me...

> I am love in you. All love in its purest form, that is Me. That is My Father. All love went into creation. All love created you and designed the plan for your life. Because of that love, I am not only the best place for you to look for help and sourcing, but also I am the only place to go. When you look to Me, I give and don't steal. I give to you according to My good plan for you, so make Me the true Lord of your life.

Lord, I appoint You as my lead, my center and my habitation. I will remain in You! I declare today: "I remain in You, Jesus. I remain in all love! There is nothing anti-love there! So, I can't hate, envy, judge, gossip or slander there. I can't walk in fear there for perfect love casts out fear. It is not in me, and I am not in fear." Lord, I give You...

Jesus says to me...

Jesus, You are Lord!

Processing His Word in His Presence

2 Corinthians 4:14-18

James 4:6-7

1 John 1:5-10

ENCOUNTER 19: LOOK TO ME

Encounter 20

We do this by keeping our eyes on Jesus, the champion who initiates and perfects our faith....

Hebrews 12:2 (NLT)

I AM YOUR SAVIOR

> Today will have a special anointing on it for peace, righteousness, joy and strength. I will direct your heart to look at Me, your eyes will drink in My love and you'll experience My outstretched hand. If you take My hand, thoughts of self-reliance will fade in our gaze. As you fall more in love with Me and with Our Father, you'll begin to see the difference as the weeks go by. You may think at times that something else has made such a difference in your thinking, stability and strength, but it's Me, Jesus. I love you, and I will take the cares from your shoulders. I am your Savior.

Jesus, You...

Jesus says to me...

" This season in your life is like a springboard. Don't be bothered by setbacks and disappointments. One change you'll notice is a new peace and perspective when circumstances don't go as you wanted or expected. It can feel like a downward motion, but it will propel you up and out. As you keep your eyes on Me, your trust will grow, and your response will increasingly come from the rested place you've found in Our fellowship."

Lord, this helps me because...

Encounter 21

Because I set you, Yahweh, always close to me, my confidence will never be weakened, for I experience your wraparound presence every moment.

Psalm 16:8 (TPT)

Processing His Word in His Presence

Hebrews 12:1-13

Psalm 24

Isaiah 35

Jesus says to me...

"Distractions will not keep My words from coming. But when you don't hear them being delivered, you will miss out on the assurance, power and advancement contained in My words. I will continue to speak, develop your faith and lead you on the path to your destiny, maturity and peace—nothing missing, nothing broken. Your perfection is not required, but the more you listen for My instructions and become aware of My voice, the easier your development and victory will be. My corrections will come to help you stay the course. I am your Savior.

Continue to meet with Me. Our times will grow more consistent until it seems We walk together without exception. Accept these words by faith, and I will bring it to pass. Seek Me early, and I will give you a new rest. I am your Savior."

You are my Savior! I seek You....

Encounter 21

Because I set you, Yahweh, always close to me, my confidence will never be weakened, for I experience your wraparound presence every moment.

Psalm 16:8 (TPT)

"Distractions will not keep My words from coming. But when you don't hear them being delivered, you will miss out on the assurance, power and advancement contained in My words. I will continue to speak, develop your faith and lead you on the path to your destiny, maturity and peace—nothing missing, nothing broken. Your perfection is not required, but the more you listen for My instructions and become aware of My voice, the easier your development and victory will be. My corrections will come to help you stay the course. I am your Savior.

Continue to meet with Me. Our times will grow more consistent until it seems We walk together without exception. Accept these words by faith, and I will bring it to pass. Seek Me early, and I will give you a new rest. I am your Savior."

*You **are** my Savior! I seek You...*

Jesus says to me...

Processing His Word in His Presence

Hebrews 12:1-13

Psalm 24

Isaiah 35

TRUST ME

> "Release the care of others into My hands. My times are coming to bear upon men's souls, which you are experiencing. It is the time of detoxification for all My people. I am flushing garbage, toxic thoughts and activities and trust mechanisms out of your life and others'. You are not only experiencing your own change, but the change in others (or lack of change) affects you as well."

Jesus says to me...

Jesus, I hear You...

"When the rich young ruler came to Me with his question, 'Good teacher, what must I do to receive eternal life?' (Mark 10:17-27), he thought I would tell him that everything he was doing was sufficient. He was surprised when I answered with the truth, and he went away sad by my path of correction. Had he not rejected my answer, he would have been joyful and forever changed.

In the same way that young man thought he knew the answer to his question, My people are asking for the glory. Yet the answer requires more than many are currently prepared to hear or to do, but I am not concerned. My grace will continue to propel and draw them to My side, little by little.

Some will jump into My presence and strip off their weights eagerly, but all My little ones will come in. It is not the Father's will that I lose even one of those He has sent Me. I am revealing My light and My glory, the glory given to Me by Our Father. His only intention was that I give it to you. For this cause, I am revealing Myself to you, but before you can fully see Me, you must see what has been hiding in you: hurts, lies from the enemy, rejection, fear, abandonment and pride. There is a long list of deceptive lies the enemy has implanted in the hearts of My people.

So, I am exposing these deceptions, pushing them to the surface, sifting them with My winnowing hand. This can cause some disturbance and confusion in you and in others until you turn to Me. So, don't be bothered by a lack of understanding in others. Simply step out of the way, watch over your own heart, listen and welcome My correction."

My Jesus, I repent for ever resisting Your help...

Jesus says to me...

> To be My disciple, My follower, and to walk in My love and grace, you must stop needing affirmation from others. This idolatry will come between My healing power and your receiving it. I am all you need. I will never reject or abandon you. I am sending My love your way every day!
>
> See Me in every manifestation of love and favor. When people tell you they are praying, it's Me. When someone encourages you, it's Me. Watch for financial blessing, gifts and services to come supernaturally and know it's Me. Settle your heart in My love. Believe it. I love *you*.

Jesus, I know You love me because...

> Be content and trust in My plan of deliverance for you. I am leading you, and you know My voice. I will make you lie down in green pastures even when you want to cry or fight back. Don't fret or worry for I've got you. I'm your salvation and champion!

You are truly my Shepherd. I trust You to...

Jesus says to me...

Processing His Word in His Presence

Malachi 4

Psalm 16

1 John 4:7-19

Encounter 22

The words I have spoken over you have already cleansed you. So, you must remain in life-union with me, for I remain in life-union with you....

John 15:3-4 (TPT)

MY SECRET GARDEN

"A gentle breeze and soft rain together are cleansing and fresh, aren't they? So are My Spirit and My Word together that uproot and blow away the chaff. The two work together to remove the old understanding, making room and preparing the ground of your heart for My truth to take root in you. You will become like a beautiful English garden. The intricate refining and pruning of your soul that happens in the secret place will create a haven, a refuge, an invitation. As others see Me at work in your life, you will open the door for them to come to Me. You will show forth My goodness and mercy as an advertisement of My peace."

Lord Jesus, when You refine and prune my soul, it brings...

" You can live at peace with others and walk in My generous and gracious love. Remember, it is My Father's love We walk in. His answer to betrayal, rejection, lack of understanding and unfaithfulness was to send Me as the messenger of His love. You have that same ability to call on Me to be His message of love to others. I am your source, and I have put My Spirit on you and in you.

Don't try to love out of your own power, with weakened, natural love! Send My love to the unlovable! I love them all! Speak life and love, speak it by faith, and I will perform it! Don't use your words against my assignment on you. I have called you to love with the love of the Father. There is no greater love or power in Heaven or earth.

Do you know I see you? Are you confident that I hear you? I will not turn you away, and I will never leave you. You can trust My love and faithfulness. Be confident in My words, 'All is well.' This is life in Our secret garden where unified purpose and understanding create the true Oneness in the Holy Spirit that My sacrifice purchased. In the days to come, no prayer of your heart will go unanswered. "

Jesus says to me...

Jesus, as I close my eyes and hear You speak, my purpose is being made one with Yours. You ask me if I know You see me and if I am confident You see me. The truth is...

> "In Our garden, these things lose their importance—entertainment, stuff, fame, riches, affirmation, prestige, renown—other than how they might serve or assist the Father and His Kingdom purpose. This life with Me is a strong foundation for peace. You can only glimpse the depth of this truth now, but it will be your great joy in days to come."

Lord, I am ready to lay down some things today...

"I am the Bread of Life, the Manna from Heaven to you, daily loading you with the good things you need for Us to do, what the Father has given Us to do. I was sent from Heaven for this purpose!

How can you join Me? What is your part?

Turn your face toward Me, precious one. Listen for My voice. Come when I call. Get up when I wake you. Wait on Me, be hungry for My Word and thirsty for My Presence. In these moments, I will reveal Myself to you and show you things to come. You won't build a garden in a day or even weeks or months. But you will grow cleaner, stronger and hungrier until this new reality with Me becomes the bedrock of your life.

When I told Peter that his life would be built on My revelation by the Spirit, he wasn't perfect in a moment either. Far from it. He needed Me and My continued loving correction and teaching for the perfecting of his life. And so do you! But here I am, and I am all yours. Don't minimize or mentally explain away this gift of My presence in your life. Just say from your soul, 'Yes, Lord!'"

Jesus, I receive the gift of Your presence! My soul says...

Jesus says to me...

Processing His Word in His Presence

1 John 5:14-15

Matthew 22:37-40

Matthew 16:13-19

Encounter 23

Could there be any other god like Yahweh? For there is not a more secure foundation than you. God, you have wrapped me in power and made my way perfect.

Psalm 18:31 (TPT)

PERFECT SECURITY

" We are in a timeshift of My Father's making. Your part in this has been established since the beginning. If you will rest in Me and My words, you'll enjoy this time.

Yes, all that can be shaken will be shaken. Though at times, you may feel the pressure of the purging, the glory will far outweigh the price. If you will look at Me—not the circumstances—you will keep your foundation established in Me. "

When I look at You, Jesus...

"When My disciples were afraid in the midst of the storm, they didn't run to Me to ask for help (Mark 4:35-41). They came to Me angry, offended and feeling abandoned. When they focused on the storm, and took their eyes off Me, they saw Me through the eyes of the storm. Had they run to Me with faith in My words and in My faithfulness, they would have seen the storm through My eyes. They would have seen the impending peace I saw.

When your eye is safely founded on truth, your whole being is sound. My disciples should have known that I would not abandon them. When you believe in Me to save, I don't merely confirm My words with signs. My words want to work *with* you, directing you, affecting your abilities, giving you peace and establishing the outcome: 'Let's go to the other side!'"

Let's go to the other side! Jesus, I'm ready to...

> I haven't changed. I want to be the One who takes you to the other side, but you must believe that the grace and power to get there are contained in My words.
>
> When you change your attention to focus on Me, I will change your ways, means and outcome. This process continues in every circumstance until you are literally changed from the inside out.
>
> Look at Me—until there is nothing else in the way. I am your Way and your Path if I am your Truth. I have Kingdom purpose for choosing you, for placing you, for keeping you in position and for moving you from glory to glory. This is not your job! So, rest and focus your attention on Me. I rested in the storm because I set My focus on My Father. Picture yourself in the storm, asleep in the boat with Me at the helm. Rest, I say!

Kellie: *Yes, Lord! What am I putting before You that causes me to see You through circumstances rather than the circumstances through You?*

Jesus says to me...

Jesus, I speak the truth to my heart. Now, I am...

"As you change focus, you will begin to know your purpose. I will redirect your priorities and bring your thoughts into alignment with My words and My will.

Without striving, you will begin to find your joy, sustenance, satisfaction, value and peace in Me. For instance, relationships can be stressful at times, requiring your attention, fixing problems and misunderstandings. When you look at loved ones through My eyes, your love for them is satisfied in Me, leaving them to see more of Me in you. Let Me direct your time, bring you favor and provide you rest. I can make certain that quality relationship time is memorable and fun! If you let Me guide and instruct you, fear of loss won't stop you from new adventures in Me. No more fear of loss, for you will now know I will see you through any trouble."

Examine my heart, Lord. I refuse to allow the fear of loss a place in my heart...

Kellie: *I declare that I am free from distractions! As in Matthew 3:16 when the dove of the Spirit rested on You, Jesus, You may rest in me because I rest in You. I will not push You away, by Your grace.*

Jesus says to me...

Processing His Word in His Presence

Matthew 3:16

Hebrews 12:18-29 MSG

Psalm 17:3-8, 15 TPT

Psalm 18:13-36 TPT

Encounter 24

Let us then approach God's throne of grace with confidence, so that we may receive mercy and find grace to help us in our time of need.

Hebrews 4:16 (NIV)

HELPING YOU

" Helping you is what I do, for grace is who I am. *Grace* is My presence of power on you to do what you cannot do. Grace is on you and in you as I am on you and in you.

Grace means I am forgiveness. I am love. I am courage. I am peace. You cannot be or do these things apart from me. This is not your part—it's My part as your Savior and Shepherd. Yours is to take from Me what is Mine and do My will, walk in My Spirit and live by My grace. Pick up My mantle and wear it. Hear My words of grace and believe and receive the power to be and do. "

Lord, I yield to Your grace as I...

> "When you allow yourself to be distracted from My words of grace, you miss out on the power contained in My *rhema* (or spoken words), and you struggle to achieve these works in yourself. Your efforts, your power, your work equals *your* results. You were made to walk in Oneness with Me and live the supernatural life that We were made to live."

Jesus says to me...

"I have set you apart to be refined in My fire. Hold nothing back from My gaze. I will work on you from the inside out, replacing stubbornness, pride, weakness and fatigue with My grace and mercy. Your struggle to overcome in practical, spiritual, emotional, physical, relational and financial matters will be forgotten as you become strong and courageous by My grace. When you are challenged, no longer think: *This can't be done*, or *What will I do?* Instead, bring it to me and exchange the care for My grace.

Even when you feel at fault for trouble or have not followed My words or will, remember My kindness toward you and come to Me."

Jesus, my Shepherd, I am tired of the struggle, so I receive Your grace and give You my cares...

Jesus says to me...

"Not only do I give you My grace, but you first have My mercy for failure and sin. When you consider mercy and grace as the same gift, you miss out on my two-step success plan for you! My goodness and mercy follow you, cleaning up your mess when you repent. But My grace is the supernatural *power* in you to overcome, succeed, finish and *win!*

So, be at peace and be still. Let Me pour My words of grace into you now. What you are facing today is no surprise to Me, and I have already won the battle for you. May I pick you up higher today and show you My grace? Your stillness allows Me entrance."

Yes! I'll be still. Take me higher...

Jesus says to me...

" Though I would fight for you if you were the only person on earth, you aren't. Realize, My love, this grace life is bigger than you or your mistakes. The Kingdom of Heaven is here, and it's you and Me, working together. Grace is the power that makes this possible! Without this supernatural merging, there will be no harvest of souls. The Kingdom of Heaven is as a farmer who needs help at the harvest. You need My help, and I need yours. I'm sending you to labor in My field. Your part is just to be available and allow My love to direct you. My power will flow through you and mercy and grace will be planted, even at times without your awareness.

Take courage. The season of change is here. My mercy hovers, and My grace flows, so take My strength and courage and go! "

Lord Jesus, I receive Your strength and courage today as I…

Processing His Word in His Presence

Hebrews 4:10-16 AMPC

Luke 1:37 AMPC

1 John 1:9

Encounter 25

I have loved you even as the Father has loved me. Remain in my love.

John 15:9 (NLT)

FAMILY LOVE

> Family love doesn't start with you but with Me. So, you only need to do your part for miraculous change. The love of the Father is irresistible. I know! You have experienced that love as We've spent time together. That same inviting love is in you, ready to flow freely to your family when unhindered and unfiltered by hurts, needs and selfish motives. When your heart is healed, it loves freely with no requirement for payback. This is how I love the world without demanding love in return. If I can love like this, you can love like this.

I will love with Your love, Jesus...

> "You have the capacity to love your worst enemy, the person who has cut you the deepest, even those who are no longer in your life because of their hurtful ways. To love like this, you have to tap directly into the flow of My love. It's not so hard to love if We are in alignment. I said to My disciples in Luke 14:26, 'If you want to be My disciple, you must, by comparison, hate everyone else—your father and mother, wife and children, brothers and sisters—yes, even your own life. Otherwise, you cannot be My disciple.'"

Kellie: *Lord, I don't think I have done that.*

Open my eyes, Lord...

"Many have not understood what I was saying, thinking they must love their loved ones less.

Understand this truth, and you will be a fountain of great love to those around you: if you want to follow Me, I must be first. How can you follow Me if you love someone else more? I don't want you to love anyone less. Just take Me from where I sit in your heart and love Me first, and you'll love Me *more*, more than anyone else.

If I am first, you will find that My love in return is the first to satisfy your need for love. You must be loved in return, but if I am your first love, that need is fully satisfied. Loving unconditionally becomes easier and easier from your satisfied soul. Loving others ceases to be about how you or they feel, but how *We love*. We don't love from necessity, control or requirement but from the well of the Father's great and unfailing love. *This* is the place of love where prayers prayed for loved ones have great power and peace.

When you love Me most, you love others best.

Can you do this today? Will you let Me judge your heart in this? For I want you to experience My love with no wall, filter or need in between. Love from an eternal fountain that flows from Heaven. Otherwise, there will come times when you cannot follow Me for you will have to follow your first loves, and My voice will dim when you need Me the most."

Lord Jesus, I choose today to love You first and most...

Jesus says to me...

> Now, *let's* pray for *Our* loved ones! Now, We pray with Matthew 18:19-20 behind us. 'If two of you agree here on earth concerning anything you ask, my Father in heaven will do it for you. For where two or three gather together as my followers, [the Greek says *gathered together in My name*] I am there among them' (NLT).
>
> These are My words, and I am also your second in agreement. When you and I agree no other agreement is needed! Write their names down, and I will give you keywords to pray, for I know them.

My loved ones are Your loved ones! Father, Jesus and I lift up...

Jesus says to me...

Processing His Word in His Presence

John 15:1-17

1 John 4:7-21

Luke 10:27

Romans 5:5

Encounter 26

Rise up in splendor and be radiant, for your light has dawned, and Yahweh's glory now streams from you!

Isaiah 60:1 (TPT)

LIGHT AND LIFE

> Day has dawned for you. There has come light to your heart. Where there was darkness, you allowed Me to cleanse you from all un-right-ness. Where there is light, there is identity, clarity and purpose that cannot be manipulated or stolen by the enemy. Light begets light! Light in one room of your heart sheds light in another room because you can now see what you were stumbling over.

Kellie: *I once was blind to the deceit hiding in my soul, but You saved me, Jesus. Thank You!*

> It was My joy to save you—the joy that was set before Me. My victorious defeat of darkness in the middle of hell itself made defeating darkness in the middle of your heart simply a matter of invitation and access. Now light has come and the glory of the Lord is rising up from within you and is beginning to flow through you. Light is a fountain of life, driving out the remaining darkness hiding in your heart.

Jesus, I thank You for...

Jesus says to me...

"I am thrilled with you and the access you've determined to give Me. I am placing new thoughts, new ideas and new Kingdom-access in your life. There is *good* ahead for you—such wonderful peace, grace, provision, impact, harmony and laughter. True laughter, born of My peace and joy, will be a marker of your new life in the days ahead. You'll notice the difference and the increase!

Enjoy the new reality of living for My purpose. Together, We are about Our Father's business. True, unshakable satisfaction will come as the Kingdom becomes the base of your life. As We bring the joy of Our Father's house to others, that joy, grace, peace and love will spread through your everyday life. Today is an open door for you, and *you* are an open door for others to see new possibilities in Me.

To be about Our Father's business, you must live in Me, remain in Me and live a face-to-face life with Me. I'm the Door to the Father, and I'm pulling you into Me. You won't get to the Father by passing through Me or walking behind Me but abiding within Me. As you *abide* in Me, you'll become increasingly established in the unshakable Kingdom! This is the light that is shining! Come in to this new day!"

As I come face to face with You, Jesus...

❝ As you walk in Me, My perfect love exposes fear and every hurtful, traumatic, implanted evil lie in your heart. Plucking the lies of the enemy out by the root system can only be done when you allow Me to have My way in your soul. Worshipping Me and putting Me first is positioning and authorizing Me for this work.

'The Lord's Prayer' is not My prayer or your prayer but OUR prayer. Every time you pray it, I am praying it. I am in you and you in Me, and this is *Our* prayer to *Our* Father. Would you pray it with Me now?

> *Our Father who art in heaven, Hallowed be thy name.*
> *Your kingdom come, Your will be done*
> *in earth, as it is in heaven.*
> *Give **us** this day **our** daily bread.*
> *And forgive **us** **our** debts, as **we** forgive **our** debtors.*
> *And lead **us** not into temptation, but deliver **us** from evil: For thine is the kingdom, and the power, and the glory, for ever. Amen.*
> Matthew 6:9-13 (KJV)

'Your Kingdom come, Your will be done' is an alignment prayer, setting things right in your heart and making new. ❞ Pray in this manner over the things that concern you.

Our Father, Jesus and I bring these concerns to You...

Processing His Word in His Presence

Psalm 19:12 TPT

Ecclesiastes 3:11-15

1 John 2

Encounter 27

> *They said to each other, "Didn't our hearts burn within us as he talked with us on the road and explained the Scriptures to us?"*
>
> Luke 24:32 (NLT)

THE LONG WALK

"In all the cleansing, let Me remind you to love yourself as I have loved you. Love yourself as you were because I did. Don't despise that person who brought you to the place where you could sit with Me now. If you don't love yourself and value your journey, the enemy will hide shame and call it righteousness.

Shame is a devilish device to convince you to hide your weaknesses instead of bringing them to Me. True conviction comes from Me, bringing a holy desire to repent and to live differently going forward. Satan would love to convince you of the impossibility of your desire to be different and open the door for shame to lodge in your soul. Shame keeps guard over your weaknesses, leaving them untouched by My hands or My miracle power. Say, 'No!' to this trickery. Give your cares and your past to Me and trust Me to heal and save you. Love all versions of yourself as My love flows into those hidden reserves."

I say "No!" to shame, Jesus. I admit to You that I...

Jesus says to me...

" I am here. Stop and sense My presence. Your weaknesses were always the open door for My power, even when you were not aware that I was working. I was and I am your Good Shepherd. Your life has been a walk with Me, and it will always be. I am here to do a quick and thorough work as We walk through a refining fire that is internal, not external—an intensity of fire like you've never known, burning the junk away. Cleansing will not always be easy, but it will be glorious and healing, bringing an intense connection with Me that will never wane. We are partners in this beautiful process. "

Jesus, in the stillness with You, I sense...

" I am restoring My hope in you, a life-altering flood of courage and a renewed expectation of divine help and victory. Hope that brings joy, peace, rest, laughter and righteousness is entering your heart as We sit together. Give Me your listening ear, and you will hear the assurance that all is well, and My peace will begin to flood your heart. No more striving, My love. My grace-power is only in the resting. Your leaning on Me becomes resting in Me, so lean in as you lay aside the weights, fears and cares. I have taken up your cause, and I am faithful to those tender treasures you place in My hands. "

Jesus says to me...

" Your soul is created to hear from Me and believe. As it is renewed and cleansed, My words, My plans and My thoughts of you will be heard. How wonderfully you've been made! How beautiful your composition! My words of love will tear down lies. My glorious light will blaze with fire, consuming every proud obstacle and stronghold in your heart. "

Jesus, I don't want anything in my heart that would be in Your way. I repent for...

> Receive today like a gift! As you receive the hope and help that I bring, realize you are in the process of becoming My perfected one. This doesn't require brilliance, perfection or rules, but it requires worship, love and humility. Come to Me, and I will give you rest; learn of Me, for I am meek and lowly of heart. I am all love, all ears and all heart for you.

Kellie: *You are welcome, my precious Savior. I receive You into the deepest place of my soul. Bring Your light and love into every corner of my heart. Be at work and be at rest in my heart. I love You, and I put my whole existence in Your loving, healing hands. I abide in You, and Your words abide in me from today forward.*

My Jesus, I come in worship, love and humility....

Jesus says to me...

Processing His Word in His Presence

2 Corinthians 12:10 TPT

Matthew 11:25-30

Luke 24:13-35

Encounter 28

For God, who said, "Let there be light in the darkness," has made this light shine in our hearts so we could know the glory of God that is seen in the face of Jesus Christ.

2 Corinthians 4:6 (NLT)

LIGHT THERAPY

"I will tell you why I have been eager for this day—the day of My unveiling—to come. When you turn to Me, the veil is removed. You are looking at Me like never before. This is the completion of Our union! Gone is the barrier that keeps My glory from shining on your face. The light that shines from My face is the creative power that glorifies your life.

My eternal essence is the glory substance that brings light to the darkness, brings the blessing and the empowerment to live, to raise the dead, to heal your body and to cleanse your soul. The light that emanates from the Father and shines from My face to yours is *everything!*

I want you to understand more fully the magnitude of what happened to Me between the cross and the resurrection. Understand that for Me to pay the penalty for your sin, I had to die. But how could I die with the absolute love and light of the Father shining on Me? The Father had no choice but to turn His face away from Me.

My Father, in whom there had never been *any* shadow of turning, looked away. It was devastating, shameful and humiliating. For three days, in the bowels of hell, there was no love, no light, no life shining on Me. So, every pain, sickness, weakness, infirmity, sin, shame, guilt and trauma that could or would ever exist, was poured into My abandoned form, unhindered by the love of the Father. Such was the enormity of the sacrifice as I set My face like a stone on the joy of presenting *you* to the Father. The Father set His face like stone *against Me.*"

Kellie: *Oh, Jesus, I'm only beginning to understand what You put aside and how You suffered for me.*

Lord, help me take this in...

"You will never know pain like that. I saw to it that no one would ever have to face total darkness, bereft of the Father's love. Only by refusing Me would anyone pay the price of hell. For there is no level of pain on earth that even comes close. On mankind's worst day, the Father still loves him. There is a degree of light that shines on the just and the unjust. But there was none for Me in those three days."

Jesus says to me...

" When you choose to turn away or look aside to any degree, you choose the veil that comes between. *Don't!* There is so much more for Us! With every consistent day of walking face to face with Me, the full force of My light comes flooding into your spirit, soul and body. My healing, provision, peace and joy ignite in Our union. I chose the darkness so you could have the light—so, please take it! "

Jesus, I choose...

> With no veil between Us, the enemy cannot convince you of abandonment or separation. My Words will bring the faith and assurance you need to stay in My presence. Be still. This is prayer without ceasing. The light, life and love of the Father are shining on you *now!* Healing is flowing as you gaze at My face and hear the words come out of My mouth. I am breathing life into your inner being. How I long to bring salvation to the details of your life!

Jesus says to me...

_____

_____

_____

_____

_____

_____

I hear You, and I believe...

_____

_____

_____

_____

_____

_____

> This is *light therapy*. My Face—the fount of fire—and My eyes—the channels of fire and the glory—are bringing life to you and death to sin! Remember: this light is not meant to be under a bushel (veiled). As you allow My light to shine on you and then shine on others, it's still My light! And this is how you heal the sick and free the captive. Let My light be yours, and let it shine!

Kellie: *I receive the light and fire that shines from Your face. I won't turn away from You, Jesus! I will shine Your light!*

Jesus, I receive…

Jesus says to me...

" Today begins a permanent impartation of *glory!*

Processing His Word in His Presence

Revelation 1:1-8

1 Corinthians 3:7-18

Luke 11:36 NLT

Encounter 29

Your people will offer themselves willingly in the day of Your power, in the beauty of holiness and in holy array out of the womb of the morning....

Psalm 110:3 (AMPC)

THE PRESS

"Good morning! No matter what time it is right now, it is morning right now in the Kingdom of God. I am waking you up all day and even in the night, to hear and understand My voice.

Today, My mercies are new and the glory is being poured out like seeing the sun shine on a beautiful day. Realize that the sun shines all the time, though your perception is affected by what is between you and the sun. Rain, clouds and storms of all kinds create the feeling of a sunless day when there is no such thing. There are only hindrances to it shining on you. Be encouraged! It is the beautiful day of My drawing near and hinderances being removed!"

Kellie: *Lord, I press into Your presence today. I love You!*

"I pressed into yours! All of hell could not keep Me from 100 percent union with you. Only you can do that. When I set My face like flint on the Father, I saw the joy that We are literally stepping into right now.

Union with you is part of that joy. The joy of pleasing My Father becomes an increasing reality as I usher you into His presence. Not only in Spirit, as you have experienced in the past, but in the days to come, you will experience Our presence in a whole new way."

Lord, I press into...

Jesus says to me...

> "I am at the doorway, as close as a guest coming into your house, stepping across the threshold. As I come closer, you will begin to have greater access to His courts. You will enter in with true praise and true worship—not in theory but in spirit and truth, reality and experience."

Jesus says to me...

"Set your face like flint on the imminent reality I have described—days of Heaven on earth. As you do, you will receive guidance, correction, power and entrance. Let the crossover begin in you. Live your life on earth in power by abiding in My presence. I will shepherd you, teach you and encourage you to be seated in your Kingdom authority and power.

Press in means more to Me than you know. Because I pressed *in*, you now can also. Just as a baby born abroad is still the citizen of the country of his parents, your citizenship is in Heaven. And just as a baby must be brought in the country by the parent, so you are being ushered in. Now You will begin to grow up in the ways of the Kingdom. I've got you! I will carry you in until you can stand in the presence on your holy feet."

Let the crossover begin, Jesus...

> "Press in. Come up. Come in and sit down with Me. For when you do, the atmosphere of Heaven will invade your atmosphere on the earth, crushing the enemy. You will walk in the truth of what I have given you, and you will have supremacy over all your circumstances. Isn't this a *joy* worth pressing into? You are worth the press. Am I?"

Jesus, You are worth...

Jesus says to me...

Processing His Word in His Presence

Psalm 110 AMPC

Isaiah 50

John 4:10-30

Luke 8:40-48

Encounter 30

In just a short time he will restore us, so that we may live in his presence. Oh, that we might know the Lord! Let us press on to know him. He will respond to us as surely as the arrival of dawn or the coming of rains in early spring.

Hosea 6:2-3 (NLT)

GATEWAY OF HOPE

"I am with you. I will respond to you. I am restoring you. Will you meet Me in this place again? Throughout this guided process, I have made promises to you, expressed My love for you and called your name, and you have done the same with Me. Do you know that I desire your presence as much as you desire Mine? I've seen that you have been unsure of My response at times, but I have watched you press in. Will you continue? 'I would rather see your love than all your sacrifices and I want you to know me more than I want an offering' (Hosea 6:7, paraphrase). I desire your attention at all times—not for Myself but so I can lead you into all the blessing and wonders I have stored up for you. Will you stay with Me? I have so much more to tell you."

Lord Jesus, I...

" When you are connected to My words, I can tell you who you truly are. When I see your face light up with the reality of your worth and significance, I begin to see Myself in your eyes. You and I are like twins—once separated. But as We are united, We realize how very much the same We are. We are heirs to the Kingdom of Heaven! I long to tell you more of your identity as a child of the Most High! Oh, the plans We have for you, for the lovers of God, and only by the Spirit of revelation can you see them. But once you see who you are to become, you cannot un-see it. We will keep looking at one another until it is evident to all that We are just like Our Father. Do you know what I love most about you? "

Jesus says to me...

Lord Jesus...

" This is not the end of a chapter or of our newfound friendship. This is the gateway to your destined place in Me. You are the gatekeeper. I am your hope, your living connection to every promise ever made to you by Father, Son and Holy Spirit. I'm your hope rope! When you hold on to Me, I am the tie from promises made to promises kept. When we are connected by this powerful hope, I can make precious promises to you, even as you walk through difficult places. Even in a season of a wilderness experience, you will be held in My hands. With every word I speak, faith will come and make a home in your heart, producing promises fulfilled—so much so that you will say what Hosea 2:15 (NLT) says:

You turned my valley of trouble into the gateway of hope! "

My Lord Jesus, You...

Jesus says to me...

"You will not recognize your life, joy or contentment in the coming days. Moreover, you will begin to perceive your true purpose and power as words of identity flow from Heaven and hit their mark in the core of your soul. Divine love, light and life will flow at a greater level than has ever been poured out on the earth. I speak to you as I spoke through Hosea, '"But then I will win her back once again. I will lead her into the desert and speak tenderly to her there. I will return her vineyards to her and transform the Valley of Trouble into a gateway of hope. She will give herself to me there, as she did long ago when she was young, when I freed her from her captivity in Egypt. When that day comes," says the Lord, "you will call me 'my husband' instead of 'my master'"' (Hosea 2:14-16 NLT).

I want to be known as the One you love, not merely the One whom you are obligated to. Abide in My presence. I will abide in yours. We will sit at the table together and work through difficult things. I will give you ideas that will come to you suddenly in a brilliant moment of light. I will only need your *'yes'* to make big things happen, for I am that God of the Bible who does what no man can do!"

My heart is so full, Jesus...

“ The greatest adventures are ahead for Us. The wide-open blank pages you face are the symbol of your new life. You, with your ear inclined toward Me, and you, a lover that responds to My invitation, *will surely* be restored in all things and live in divine friendship with Me. Blank lines are the promised land of My presence. Let's fill them up and never stop. ”

Processing His Word in His Presence

Hosea 2, 14 NLT

Romans 5:1-11 TPT

Psalm 63

Psalm 78:1-2

Psalm 25:14-16 TPT

THE BLANK LINES AHEAD

I hope you see now that the purpose of this guided journal was not for you to learn from my conversations with the Lord but for you to respond to His invitation to enjoy conversations with Him for the rest of your life!

Jesus has only just begun to shepherd you into His plan for you. As you move on to the beautifully blank lines ahead, remember why you sat down with Him in the first place. Was it to know His thoughts for you and about you? Was it to grow closer to Him and understand His Word? Was it to begin to hear His voice for yourself?

Are you satisfied now, or are you hungrier for His presence than ever? I have found that the more of Him I experience, the more of Him I need and want. First John 3:1-3 (TPT) expresses how I feel after walking and talking with Him the last few years:

> *Look with wonder at the depth of the Father's marvelous love that he has lavished on us! He has called us and made us his very own beloved children. The reason the world doesn't recognize who we are is that they didn't recognize him. Beloved, we are God's children right now; however, it is not yet apparent what we will become. But we do know that when it is finally made visible, we will be just like him, for we will see him as he truly is. And all who focus their hope on him will always be purifying themselves, just as Jesus is pure.*

You are being revealed even now. Imagine that on the blank lines ahead profound mysteries are already written in the invisible ink of

1 Corinthians 2:6-16 (TPT), just waiting to be illuminated by the Spirit.

> *However, there is a wisdom that we continually speak of when we are among the*
>
> *spiritually mature. It's wisdom that didn't originate in this present age, nor did it come*
>
> *from the rulers of this age who are in the process of being dethroned. Instead,*
>
> *we continually speak of this wonderful wisdom that comes from God, hidden before*
>
> *now in a mystery. It is his secret plan, destined before the ages, to bring us into glory.*
>
> *None of the rulers of this present world order understood it, for if they had, they*
>
> *never would have crucified the Lord of shining glory. This is why the Scriptures say:*
>
> *Things never discovered or heard of before, things beyond our ability to imagine —*
>
> *these are the many things God has in store for all his lovers. But God now unveils these*
>
> *profound realities to us by the Spirit. Yes, he has revealed to us his inmost heart and*
>
> *deepest mysteries through the Holy Spirit, who constantly explores all things.*
>
> *After all, who can really see into a person's heart and know his hidden impulses*
>
> *Except for that person's spirit? So it is with God. His thoughts and secrets*

*are only fully understood by his Spirit, the
Spirit of God. For we did not
receive the spirit of this world system but the Spirit of God,
so that we might come to understand and experience
all that grace has lavished upon us.
And we articulate these realities with the words imparted
to us by the Spirit and not with the words taught by
human wisdom. We join together Spirit-revealed truths
with Spirit-revealed words. Someone living on an entirely
human level rejects the revelations of God's Spirit,
for they make no sense to him. He can't
understand the revelations of the Spirit
because they are only discovered by the illumination
of the Spirit. Those who live in the
Spirit are able to carefully evaluate all
things, and they are subject to the
Scrutiny of no one but God. For Who has
ever intimately known the mind of
the Lord Yahweh well enough to become
his counselor? Christ has,
and we possess Christ's perceptions.*

Imagine what is written on these lines consists of what you are to become. As it is made visible to you by the Spirit, you will see that you are just like Him.

Second Corinthians 3:16-18 (TPT) says:

*But the moment one turns to the Lord with an
open heart, the veil is lifted and they see.*

> *Now, the "Lord" I'm referring to is the Holy Spirit, and wherever he is Lord, there is freedom. We can all draw close to him with the veil removed from our faces. And with no veil we all become like mirrors who brightly reflect the glory of the Lord Jesus. We are being transfigured into his very image as we move from one brighter level of glory to another. And this glorious transfiguration comes from the Lord, who is the Spirit.*

You have spent this time turned toward the face of Jesus, experiencing His presence. The veil has been lifted from your eyes, and freedom has come for you to now see what you are to become.

The more you look at Him, the more He is revealed. And the more He is revealed. the more *you* are revealed! Continue to look at Him, and you'll continue to have an ear to hear. It is becoming more and more apparent and visible that you have been with Jesus.

SEATED IN HIS LOVE

I want to encourage you with some words from the bride in Song of Songs (Song of Solomon) 7:10-8:2a (TPT):

> *Now I know that I am for my beloved and all his desires are fulfilled in me. Come away, my lover. Come with me to the faraway fields. We will run away together to the forgotten places and show them redeeming love. Let us arise and run*

to the vineyards of your people and see if the budding vines of love are now in full bloom. We will discover if their passion is awakened. There I will display my love for you. The love apples are in bloom, sending forth their fragrance of spring. The rarest of fruits are found at our doors—the new as well as the old.

I have stored them for you, my lover-friend!

If only I could show everyone this passionate desire I have for you. If only I could express it fully, no matter who was watching me, without shame or embarrassment. I long to bring you to my innermost chamber—this holy sanctuary you have formed within me. O that I might carry you within me!

The bride, knowing she *belongs* to him, cries out to be able to fully express her love for him. In her yearning for her love, she has sought out the old and new fruit he provides. Her love for him erases shame and embarrassment, allowing the space in her heart to enlarge so she would be able to carry him within.

Amazingly, Jesus has offered us a relationship as precious and intimate as a marriage. He wants nothing less than an intimacy built on the complete giving of ourselves to Him even as He has given Himself to us. I realize this becomes uncomfortable to think about until you realize truly there is no male or female factor in this love relationship with Him. He simply wants our whole heart in the sense of knowing us intimately—every place in us we like and every place we would like to cover up. No matter who you are—male or female—you are becoming part of His Bride and becoming one with His heart. And He is one with you. If you are willing, hear His call as you read on.

The King responds with great joy. He knows you and calls you by name, thrilled by your newfound dependence on Him. He's awakened you and will continue to birth a new faith in you for a new glory and fire as you continue to fix your eyes on Him. This living, consuming flame will seal you as His forever.

Read with me in Song of Songs (Song of Solomon) 8:5-7 (TPT):

> *Who is this one? She arises out of her desert, clinging to her beloved.*
>
> *When I awakened you under the apple tree, as you were feasting upon me,*
>
> *I awakened your innermost being with the travail of birth as you longed for more of me. Fasten me upon your heart as a seal of fire forevermore.*
>
> *This living, consuming flame will seal you as my prisoner of love.*
>
> *My passion is stronger than the chains of death and the grave, all consuming as the very flashes of fire from the burning heart of God.*
>
> *Place this fierce, unrelenting fire over your entire being. Rivers of pain and persecution will never extinguish this flame. Endless floods will be unable to quench this raging fire that burns within you. Everything will be consumed.*
>
> *It will stop at nothing as you yield everything to this furious fire until it won't even seem to you like a sacrifice anymore.*

Did you think He would stop talking to you? No! He has begun a work of love in you, and He will continue it. He will stop at nothing to bring to pass His promises to you. Does it even feel like a sacrifice anymore to sit with Him and hear of His love and plans for you?

PROMISES TO TAKE YOU DEEPER

Communion with Jesus stays simple when we stay simple.

Psalm 19:7 (NLT) says:

> *The instructions of the Lord are perfect, reviving the soul.*
> *The decrees of the Lord are trustworthy, making wise the simple.*

Continue to be simple before the Lord, and position yourself as a simple listener with an ear to hear, a simple follower with a heart to do and a simple vessel for Him to pour Himself into. In the lines ahead and the days and weeks ahead, He will make you wise, joyous and beloved. He will load you up with His words of grace, power, love and healing as you listen and lean on His words.

Psalm 16:6-11 (NKJV) promises:

> *The lines have fallen to me in pleasant places;*
> *Yes, I have a good inheritance.*
> *I will bless the Lord who has given me counsel;*
> *My heart also instructs me in the night seasons.*
> *I have set the Lord always before me;*
> *Because He is at my right hand I shall not be moved.*
> *Therefore my heart is glad, and my glory rejoices;*

> *My flesh also will rest in hope.*
> *For You will not leave my soul in Sheol,*
> *Nor will You allow Your Holy One to see corruption.*
> *You will show me the path of life;*
> *In Your presence is fullness of joy;*
> *At Your right hand are pleasures forevermore.*

Some words for you from Ephesians 5:8-19(TPT):

> *Once your life was full of sin's darkness, but now you have the very light of our Lord shining through you because of your union with him. Your mission is to live as children flooded with his revelation-light! And the supernatural fruits of his light will be seen in you—goodness, righteousness, and truth. Then you will learn to choose what is beautiful to our Lord. And don't even associate with the servants of darkness because they have no fruit in them; instead, reveal truth to them. The very things they do in secret are too vile and filthy to even mention. Whatever the revelation-light exposes, it will also correct, and everything that reveals truth is light to the soul. This is why the Scripture says,*
>
> *"Arise, you sleeper! Rise up from your coffin and the Anointed One will shine his light into you!" So be very careful how you live, not being like those with no understanding, but live honorably with true wisdom, for we are living in evil times. Take full advantage of every day as you spend your life for his purposes.*
>
> *And don't live foolishly for then you will have discernment to fully understand God's will. And don't get drunk with wine, which is rebellion; instead be filled continually with*

the Holy Spirit. And your hearts will overflow with a joyful song to the Lord. Keep speaking to each other with words of Scripture, singing the Psalms with praises and spontaneous songs given by the Spirit!

Wake up! He is shining His light on you more and more as you run toward Him. It's only the beginning of your experiences with Him.

Oh, the places He will take you as you walk face to face, hand in His, through the open door…

But the path of the righteous is like the light of dawn, which shines brighter and brighter until full day.

Proverbs 4:18 (ESV)

ASK JESUS INTO
Your Heart!

If you've never personally asked Jesus to be your Lord and Savior, I invite you to pray this prayer aloud with me now. It will be the best decision of your life—and the first step toward *experiencing* His presence and enjoying intimate encounters with Jesus.

> Father, Your Word says, *"Everyone who calls on the name of the Lord will be saved"* (Acts 2:21, NLT). So, I call on You now. Take my life and do something beautiful with it.
>
> I believe Your Word that says if I confess with my mouth that Jesus is Lord and believe in my heart that You have raised Him from the dead, I will be saved (Romans 10:9-10).
>
> Jesus, come into my heart. I believe in my heart and confess with my mouth that You were raised from the dead. I invite You to be My Lord and Savior. Thank You for forgiving me of all my sins.
>
> I am now a new person inside! (2 Corinthians 5:17). You gave Your life for me, and now I live mine for You. In Jesus' name, amen.

If you've prayed this prayer today,
share your good news with me
@ kelliecopeland.com/salvation.

ABOUT THE AUTHOR

Kellie Copeland

Author · Speaker · Entrepreneur · TV Host

Raised in the loving, faith-filled home of ministers Kenneth and Gloria Copeland, Kellie experienced unique ministry training and witnessed firsthand the faithfulness of Jesus. A lifetime of living by faith equipped her to face difficult times that came her way and paved the way for Jesus to become her everything.

Kellie's passion to know Jesus more intimately has created an atmosphere for transparent conversations and ministry opportunities on her weekly talk show *Kellie* on the Victory Channel.

She is the author of *Protecting Your Family in Dangerous Times* and impacts children around the world as Commander Kellie of Superkid Academy.

Kellie's full-time love is her family. She is living her best life with Emily, her youngest daughter, and last gift at home. The Texas grandmommy of five also loves to spend as much time as she can with her four grown children and their amazing spouses.

For more information, visit
http://kelliecopeland.com/awake